1894: EUROPEAN THEATRE IN TURMOIL

Meaning and Significance of the Theatre a Hundred Years Ago

Edited by

Hub. Hermans, Wessel Krul, Hans van Maanen

Amsterdam - Atlanta, GA 1996

Senior editorial assistant: Marijke Wubbolts
Cover Designer: Peggy Vogel
Cover-photo:
Pinero's *The second Mrs. Tanqueray.* Act I of the original production with
Mrs. Patrick Campbell and George Alexander, from *The Graphic* (1893).

♾ The paper on which this book is printed meets the requirements of "ISO
9706:1994, Information and documentation - Paper for documents -
Requirements for permanence".

CIP-GEGEVENS KONINKLIJKE BIBLIOTHEEK, DEN HAAG

1894

1894: European theatre in turmoil : Meaning and
significance of the theatre a hundred years ago /
ed. by Hub. Hermans, Wessel Krul, Hans van Maanen. —
Amsterdam - Atlanta, GA 1996 : Rodopi
Proceedings of a conference held at Groningen University
in March 1994. (Tijdschrift voor Theaterwetenschap : 36)
ISBN: 90-5183-931-6
NUGI 925
Trefw.: theaterbedrijf ; Europa ; geschiedenis ; 1894-1994.

©Editions Rodopi B.V., Amsterdam - Atlanta, GA 1996
Printed in The Netherlands

Contents

PREFACE

This volume contains the proceedings of a conference held at Groningen University in March 1994. Under the title 'European Theatre in Turmoil: Meaning and Significance of the Theatre a Hundred Years Ago', an international group of scholars addressed a variety of problems connected with the different directions in European theatre in and around the year 1894. From the outset, it was decided not to limit the conference to only one literary movement, style of acting or theatrical genre, let alone to one country. Tradition and avant-garde, high and low culture, major events and secondary developments, should be equally represented. The choice of the year 1894 as the focus of the conference was therefore determined by an attempt to start on neutral ground, without any preconceived ideas: if one could go back exactly a hundred years in time, what would be the most striking aspects that presented themselves in a survey of the theatre in Europe?

But even if the historical date was to a certain extent arbitrarily chosen, this does not mean that the conference lacked a unifying theme. The early 1890s indeed marked a turning-point in European theatrical culture. The contributions to the conference, concerned as they were with totally different aspects of the theatrical arts, have made this abundantly clear. With regard to the theatre, the decisive trend of the epoch should not be sought in the rise and dominance of a certain literary theory or in an abrupt change in the style of acting and directing. Realism and naturalism, which had themselves only recently been introduced to the theatre, were in the 1890s joined by symbolism. But this new movement never entirely replaced its slightly older counterpart. Until well into the twentieth century both conceptions existed side by side. The intensity of the debate that accompanied this development, however, is indicative of an underlying, persistent tendency, that proved to be of enormous importance for the future. This tendency can be described as a growing seriousness in attitude towards the theatre.

The fact that the theatre, much more than before, began to be seen as a form of serious entertainment, influenced the art in almost every way. Its consequences were often, even mainly, beneficial. Nevertheless, we are now, after a century, also more aware of its disadvantages. Until the 1880s, the new repertoire almost everywhere in Europe was dominated by the *pièce bien faite*, the 'well-made' play according to a formula of mainly French origin. This genre has often, and not without justice, been condemned as a preeminently bourgeois type of theatre. It meant, after all, no more than to provide an evening of light amusement 'entre les plaisirs de la table et ceux du lit'. The idea of the theatre as an institution catering for a simply pleasure-seeking audience, however, ensured that it maintained certain ties with popular culture. The well-made play, with its sentimental and frequently implausible plot, could, in principle, be enjoyed by a very large segment of society. There was no strict dividing line between the bourgeois repertoire and the so-called 'lower' forms of entertainment, such as the vaudeville, revue and cabaret.

Most European theatres offered, apart from the main seating area, cheap seats or standing places for those who had only little to spend.

In the later nineteenth century the different theatrical genres were much more strongly demarcated. The high seriousness which had until then been the preserve of the history play and the tragedy, now invaded the bourgeois theatre as such. Several mutually reinforcing factors contributed to this development. The economic recession of the years between 1873 and 1895 widened the gap between the well-to-do and the working classes. In many parts of Europe, the recession also intensified the migration to the towns. Almost everywhere the urban bourgeoisie became the conspicuous ruling class. It tried hard to live up to this role. The great urban developments of the era invariably included, among the monumental buildings destined to symbolize its rise to power, one or more new theatre-houses. These were not only bigger, more luxurious and better equipped than their predecessors, they also served a moral purpose. They were intended, by their style and decoration, to demonstrate the dignity and the responsability of the social elite. Inevitably, this function was reflected in the choice of repertoire. The search for social distinction led, at least among part of the audience, to a search for more refined forms of entertainment. The growing number of 'respectable' women that visited the theatre was another indication of a gradual change in values.

The rise of the bourgeois theatre had some predictable and some unexpected consequences. Its productions became more expensive and more elevated in tone. There was little room left for a lower-class audience. The actors and playwrights, as far as they made their name on the big stages, could only gain by this narrowing of the social sphere in the theatre. Their status and income underwent a marked amelioration. From being a generally despised profession, acting became a way to sometimes very real social advancement. Around the turn of the century, it was no longer totally unacceptable for sons and daughters of the upper middle class to seek a career on the stage. The theatre came to be regarded with all the respect that was due to a form of high art.

Thus, on the stage, the moral seriousness of bourgeois life was enacted to a largely bourgeois audience. It was sometimes difficult to see where the stage ended and daily life began. At first, the manners and opinions of the middle class were taken to the theatre, but soon various theatrical attitudes and intentions began to pervade life itself. The transference of role-playing from a closed to an open audience is one of the characteristic traits of late nineteenth-century society. Every public meeting became an occasion for theatrical effects. Not only politics, but also science and the law were conducted along dramatic lines. Scientists and medical professors — Charcot in Paris is the best-known example — demonstrated their conclusions as if they were part of a carefully staged performance. The great trials and law cases of the era were reported from day to day in the press as if the participants, in the dialogue of interrogation and in their long dramatic monologues, were literally actors.

In the long run, however, the new seriousness that the middle class had brought to the theatre, turned against itself. The theatrical, 'spectacular', presentation of life both on the stage and in the public arena made it easier to see the whole of bourgeois morality as a kind of acting, and therefore as essentially untruthful. Moreover, the importance accorded to the moral and educational function of the theatre almost automatically invited a constant reconsideration and revaluation of its basic values. If the theatre should not just entertain, but direct the thought of the audience to serious considerations, the various conflicts in public morality could not be left aside. It soon appeared that these conflicts were often difficult to resolve without questioning the entire validity of bourgeois culture. Every attempt at a serious depiction of middle-class life ran the risk of turning into social criticism. In this way, the roles came to be radically reversed: while originally the theatre sought to portray the outward forms of social life, in the end life itself was seen as playing the theatre, and it was the stage that became the place of social and psychological truth.

This striving for truth beyond the accepted conventions of middle-class social life underlies both naturalism and symbolism. In the early 1890s, the theatre almost everywhere in Europe tried to free itself of the limitations imposed by the tradition of the 'well-made' play. This could be done by satire, as in the plays of Oscar Wilde and the early one-act plays by Chekhov, by an immediate attack on bourgeois morality, as in Ibsen and Strindberg, or by a total rejection of the illusion of reality on the stage. With Maeterlinck's *Les aveugles* (1891) the concept of avant-garde theatre was introduced, that became of fundamental importance for the twentieth century. Alfred Jarry's *Ubu roi* (1896) has by now become one of the classics of the modern tradition. We must be aware, however, that the avant-garde theatre was only partly successful in regaining the popular appeal of earlier forms of the theatre. That the new seriousness also entailed a loss is shown by the examples given in this collection from Spain and Germany. The effects of the new directions of the 1890s are still very much with us today.

The editors wish to express their thanks to Ms Marijke Wubbolts for her invaluable help in organizing the conference and in the preparation of this volume.

Hans van Maanen
TEXT AND THEATRE

The theme of this volume, 'Meaning and Significance in the Theatre a Hundred Years Ago', seems to be a very complex one, because several terms within the theme can be understood in very different ways by people who come from many different academic disciplines. This holds true in the first place for the term 'theatre', but in some measure also for the words 'meaning' and 'significance'.

To start with the term 'theatre', I would like to emphasize that the title of this conference is not European *drama* in turmoil, although, without any doubt, drama also was in turmoil in most European countries at the end of the nineteenth century. But, when we speak of theatre, we are embracing a whole field of theatrical genres, such as opera, dance, cabaret and what we call in the Dutch language 'toneel', but what in English can be called 'drama' or perhaps 'spoken theatre'. This field of theatre is demonstrated in a first diagram:

Diagram 1. The field of theatre

I agree with Bernard Beckerman[1] that one of the characteristics which all species in this field have in common, is that they all rely on direct communication between performers and spectators, in other words, they are performing arts. But, not all performing arts can be considered to belong to this field of theatre, because a second characteristic is, that the human body is the dominant instrument used in the performance. That is the reason why for instance a great number of music performances cannot be scheduled in the field of theatre.

A third characteristic concerning different kinds of theatre, is that they do not necessarily need to be dramatical. Cabaret, rope-walking, some sorts of dance are not dramatical, although they are theatrical. These theatrical, but non-dramatical genres lack characteristics of drama, especially what Beckerman called 'the imagined act'.

Martin Esslin approached the question of theatre and drama from a totally different side. In his small book *The Field of Drama* he stated that drama today plays a more important role in our lives than it ever did. I quote:

> Drama, there can be no doubt about it, has become immensely important in our time. More human beings than ever before see more drama than ever before and are more directly influenced, conditioned and programmed by drama than ever before. Drama has become one of the principal vehicles of information, one of the prevailing methods of 'thinking' about life and its situations.[2]

The reason why Esslin can make this statement, is clear: it is because film and television drama have taken over the traditional functions of drama on stage and have multiplied the possible dramatic experiences out of all proportion.

So, if we follow Martin Esslin, next to the field of theatre, a field of drama can be defined also, including television drama, film, video and stage drama.

Diagram 2. The field of drama

It is not very difficult to see that these two fields — theatre and drama — demonstrate an overlap and that we will find drama on stage, of course, in the centre of this overlap.

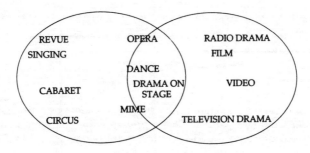

Diagram 3. Overlap of the fields of theatre and drama

Although Theatre Studies broke away from the study of literature — a hundred years ago indeed — we can conclude that a great part of Theatre Studies is concerned with drama on stage, and especially drama on stage, based on drama texts which are canonized as important literary works. The latter is not very surprising because a certain relationship can be assumed between the level of significance of a performance and the level of significance of the text used. This is so even when on the one hand this relationship is not a fixed one and on the other hand a lot of brilliant performances have been made on the basis of unimportant texts. Meanwhile dance is the only performing art that, besides drama on stage, has achieved a structural place in a number of institutes for Theatre Studies. Another development causing the borders between the field of drama and the field of theatre to blur, is that theatre researchers started to include studies of film and television drama over the last ten years.[3]

The main point of difference between the literary and the theatrical approach, however, is that they have different objects of study. Literary people study the drama text in essence as a literary artefact, or also the possible or realised reception of a text by readers. Theatre researchers on the other hand take the performance as such as their object of study, meaning, strictly speaking, the possible or realised artistic communication between performers and audience on the basis of the presentation by the performers. Clearly the words 'drama' or 'drama text' do not appear in this description of the object at all. This difference has important consequences for the kinds of questions asked, which is demonstrated in the diagram below.

Themes and Thoughts in a Dramatic Structure

CHARACTERS   ACT   in   SITUATIONS ——→ CONFLICTS

Diagram 4. Simplified structure of a drama text

This diagram can be considered as a simplified model of a dramatic text. Themes, ideas, thoughts, and so on are present within a dramatic structure which can be characterized by four terms: characters which act in situations resulting in developing conflicts. A second diagram shows the possible relations between readers and such a text.

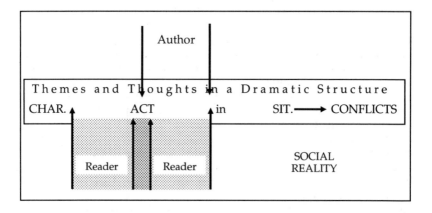

Diagram 5. The relation between readers and a dramatic text

What we see first of all is that each reader has a very direct relationship to the text, secondly that this relationship is coloured by the social reality each reader lives in, and thirdly, of course, that the mental systems of the different readers overlap each other more or less. The object of the literary study of a drama text can be:

1. the text as such; 2. the origin of the text; or 3. the reading of it. To do some research into the third possibility it should be worthwhile to study the mental systems of the readers and the ways in which they influence the reading process.

When we move to the approach of Theatre Studies, we can start with the same model of themes and thoughts in a dramatic structure, and the communication process (between actors and audience). In his effort to enter into the dramatic core however, the spectator has to go through two other structures in which the dramatic structure itself is implied.

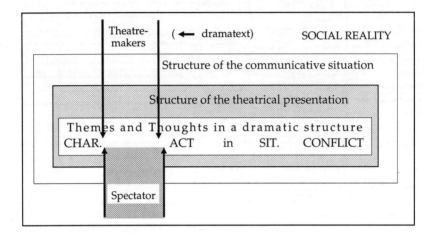

Diagram 6. Relation between spectator and drama

It can be inferred from this diagram, that there are not only two levels between the spectator and the dramatic structure, but, more importantly, the core objective of the theatre researcher can no longer be found in the dramatic structure itself, but in the structure of the theatrical presentation, the performance and sometimes especially in the small shaded block where the spectator meets the performance. This change in the object of study is caused by the fact that in a performance the dramatic structure does not have an independent existence, but can only be experienced *through* or rather *in* the wider structure of the performance as a whole. More to the point, this means that a spectator is communicating with actors, on the basis of their presentation, and the dramatic text as such does not play any part in that communication-process at all. In other words: from the point of view of theatre studies, theatre is considered a creative, not a recreative form of art.

I know that from a literary point of view some colleagues plead for different approach, namely that a theatre performance is a process of communication between the author and the audience through the mediation of a theatre company. I have experienced this myself, when I, some years ago, tried to explain to students in the Department of Literature Studies how I — as a director of a company — had modified a play written by Ibsen (whose texts I admire), in order to use that text for my own theatrical purposes. Only disbelief and anger did I encounter for my trouble.[4]

Also, it must be noted that a reader finds him- or herself in a specific situation which has its influence on both the reader and the reading. But in general this situation is a personal matter and has no direct influence on the book itself.

In theatre, on the other hand, plays can only be performed in specific ways, in specific buildings or situations and spectators have to make their own way to these places. It will be clear that those locations as such do therefore influence the theatre-making as well as the theatre-watching, as is directly visible when other places, moments or locations are chosen or created by theatre companies to communicate with an audience. This communicative situation is in essence a socially organised situation, an institutional one, if you want, which means that the theatrical communication between spectators and actors can be studied as a socially *organised* process.

Meaning and significance of drama originate in principle through performances. One of the best examples is the history of *The Seagull* by Chekhov, which, although first staged in 1896, achieved its modern meaning by Stanislawsky's method of staging from 1898 onwards.

An important aim of the conference, on which this book is based, was to search for the kinds of meanings that theatre created and communicated at the end of the nineteenth century, and also the significance it had, through these diverse meanings, in the European societies of the time.

Meanings of artistic works are, like all meanings, the outcomes of a process. Meaning is produced in this process by different instances at different stages. Firstly, it mostly is an author who creates meanings by writing a play, in which he uses his social environment as input, especially his personal experience with it. The play, in turn, forms as a sign-system one of the inputs for the theatre-makers (besides *their* own experience of the social environment), who produce meanings again within their own sign-systems: thus we get the performance. This performance, finally, functions as input in the reception-process in which the spectators produce their own meanings.

Not only the production of meanings themselves at the different stages, but also their significance in society at large, will depend on the institutional conditions under which these meanings are produced, in other words under which the play and the performance are produced and received.

This means, the other way around, that the significance, let us say the importance to be clear, of the theatre as such in a given period, will determine the significance of meanings produced in this theatre. If we may believe some spokesmen of the late nineteenth century, the significance of the theatre in a quantitative and in a qualitative sense was not to be underestimated. In Berlin and Copenhagen invitations for societies and parties were accompanied by the explicit request not to speak about the play *Nora* by Ibsen, and Conrad Alberti speaks of a *Nora*-mania during some weeks in the families of some districts of Berlin. To render explicable how theatre can function in such a way, I worked out a small model, in which I could split up the

question of how meanings are produced in theatre into twelve fields which
correspond with the different stages I wrote about earlier.

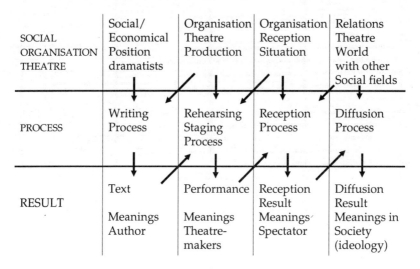

SOCIAL ORGANISATION THEATRE	Social/ Economical Position dramatists	Organisation Theatre Production	Organisation Reception Situation	Relations Theatre World with other Social fields
PROCESS	Writing Process	Rehearsing Staging Process	Reception Process	Diffusion Process
RESULT	Text Meanings Author	Performance Meanings Theatre-makers	Reception Result Meanings Spectator	Diffusion Result Meanings in Society (ideology)

Diagram 7. Production of meaning in a theatre world

From left to right the model demonstrates the production of meanings in
succession: text, performance, perception and ideology. In each column we
find the three stages of social conditions, production process and the result
of each process. The small arrows finally indicate the main influences of
some fields on others.

The articles in this collection cover very different areas of this scheme. I can
imagine, for instance, that literary people will especially contribute to the
understanding of the first column; this will be very important to the theatre
researchers too, because they have left these fields more or less, during the
last twenty-five years, to engage themselves more in the fields of the second
and the third columns, performance analysis and reception research. The
fourth column appears to be reserved for a more theatre-sociological
approach.

As is very apparent in my model, the various approaches need each other,
not only because of the mutual influences involved, but also because all the
distinguished fields exist and function in a social reality that will influence
them all.

Notes

1. B. Beckerman, *Dynamics of drama*. New York, 1970.

2. M. Esslin, *The Field of Drama* (London, 1987), p. 13.

3. But if we look at the program of the festival held during the conference, on which these articles are based, it appears that the four groups from university theatre departments played Wedekind, Strindberg, Feydeau and Heijermans; the Russian actors played Chekhov and only from Spain and Great-Britain non-literary based theatre was performed.

4. Another example of this phenomenon occurred some time ago in one of the small theatres in Groningen. To close a workshop on play-writing for beginning authors, one of the plays was performed by Jack Nieborg. The play was about the cramped relation between a middle-aged woman and her family. The director chose for the four roles four children of nine years old who recited the play pretty well, while in the background a fake audience little by little left the auditorium. It was a fascinating performance, but the author was not very happy with the way in which the meanings of her play had been conveyed.

Helen Wilcox
'THE WEEPING AND THE LAUGHTER':
SOME ENGLISH LITERARY THOUGHTS ON THE 1890s

> Suit the action to the word, the word to the action, with this special
> observance, that you o'erstep not the modesty of nature. For anything
> so o'erdone is from the purpose of playing, whose end both at the first
> and now was and is, to hold as 'twere the mirror up to nature; to
> show virtue her own feature, scorn her own image, and the very age
> and body of the time his form and pressure. (*Hamlet* 3.2.15-20)

We could do a lot worse than to begin our consideration of European Theatre
in 1894 with Shakespeare. Not that Shakespeare had any particular connection with the year in question — other than that his plays were being
performed then on many European stages in a variety of languages — but his
texts have much to say on the power and danger of theatre which is
undoubtedly relevant to our discussions. In his conversations with the group
of actors who visit Elsinore, Hamlet highlights the ambivalence of the
theatrical phenomenon. On the one hand it is, after all, a mere falseness — an
unreal 'fiction', a "dream of passion" (2.2.504) — phrases evoking the dread
of the element of pretence and impersonation which is always present in
attacks on the dangerous illusion of theatre. But this apparent 'fiction' creates
(in Hamlet's strikingly immediate metaphor) a "false fire" (3.2.241) which can
"fright" those who see it, threatening them with a force akin to that of real
fire. It is exciting, powerful, disturbing, and can burn those who play with
it. On the other hand, the theatre can use its influence benevolently and
constructively. A play, when "set down with as much modesty as cunning",
can in Hamlet's view be most "excellent" (2.2.399-400), entertaining finely
with wit, beauty and honesty. As is suggested by Hamlet in the passage
which I quoted in full above, the major purpose of playing is to create, not
illusions, but home truths: to "hold as 'twere the mirror up to nature", show
"virtue her own feature", show "scorn her own image" and present to "the
very age and body of the time, his form and pressure" (3.2.18-20). This
reference to the 'time' as contained and expressed in the theatre echoes
another phrase of Hamlet's, in which he describes the players as "abstract
and brief chronicles of the time" (2.2.481-2) who can vividly epitomise an age.
Theatre, then, has ambiguous powers: it works at the level of 'fiction' or
'dream', and yet is a 'mirror' giving an accurate reflection of an individual,
a type, or an era of history. The players acting in a drama represent created
personalities but present in their brief time on the stage an 'abstract' or
summary of a longer work of historical time; they embody and give
chronicling voice to a sequence of events. Thus it is, then, that we hope to
understand more about Europe in 1894 by looking at the nature of theatre in
that year — as well as hoping to learn more about theatre by looking at it in

the contextualising colours of the 1890s. Why was it that European theatre was so vibrant in this period, with the Théâtre Libre in Paris, Shaw and Wilde in London, Yeats in Ireland, Ibsen and Strindberg to the north and Chekhov and Stanislavski at the Moscow Arts Theatre to the east? We may find in the theatrical history of 1894 a lively 'mirror' of the year and of theatre — but we must remember that a mirror image *is* only an image, and may well, like theatre itself, mislead us with its powers of fantasy and illusion.

When we begin to look into the last decade of the nineteenth century, we find that the 'mirror' can indeed present a disconcertingly slanted image. Have we strayed from the theatre into a fairground with its hall of teasing, distorting mirrors? Our first impression is of the difficulty of seeing the 'real' 1890s through the images of the era that we have inherited. Misleading myths of the '90s abound (as we in the 1990s should be well aware): we have a generalised impression of the 1890s as an era of decadence and perhaps even deviance, summed up in the term 'naughty nineties'. Such catch-phrases, of course, are unsubtle, and in their mockery can offer too easy a way out, a belittling summary which renders the radical challenges of the age safely invisible. We should be put on our guard by the fact that this image of a decadent end of the century was satirised just as soon as the decade began, in a parody of the literary decadents written by Lionel Johnson in 1891:

> We are the elect of Beauty: saints and sinners, devils and devotees, Athenians and Parisians, Romans of the Empire and Italians of the Renaissance. Fin de siecle! Fin de siecle! Literature is a thing of beauty, blood and nerves. (Thornton 1970: 22)

This merciless mockery of decadent 'devotees' of art and indulgence, by an immediate contemporary, should make us wary of accepting the myth of the self-indulgent '90s too readily. However, it gives us some important clues towards a more accurate picture of the era. First, it is a European vision, toying with extremes of saintliness and sinfulness but drawing an impressive range of civilisations — Athenian and Roman, Parisian and Italian — into its mock coterie. This is an apt reminder of the international nature of culture, including the theatrical, in the 1890s, a phenomenon which we are struggling to parallel with political unity in the 1990s. Second, the terms used to describe literature in Johnson's parody are bodily — 'blood and nerves' — reminding us that this was an age of sensual rather than wholly cerebral responses. We have only to recall, for example, the physicality of paintings in this period depicting the crowded bars and concert-halls of Paris. Johnson's parody is itself also unashamedly art-focussed; earlier in same piece he mocks the imagined decadent who claims that 'we alone know beauty and art' (as well as 'sorrow and sin'). This highlights a third quality of the 1890s, its emphasis on art and the artificial. As Oscar Wilde summed it up, 'the first duty in life is to be as artificial as possible'. Arthur Symons, defining the decadent movement in literature in 1893 and linking it with symbolism and impressionism, commented that the function of the arts, as exemplified in the poetry of Verlaine, was to "fix the last fine shade, the quintessence of things; to fix it fleetingly" (Thornton: 29). This stress on the stopping of flux, however briefly, by means of art, returns us to the nature of theatre: it is a frame which fixes, if only for a moment, the essence of an era.

As we strive to understand the 1890s through the distorted frames of reference that we have at our disposal — catch-phrases, myths, parodies, painted self-images, theories both then and now — some elements are beginning to emerge: decadence and physicality; Europeanness; art for art's sake. To these we must add the sense of an ending, typical of the final decade of any century but particularly crucial in the 1890s which came at a late stage in Victorianism and in the fortunes of the British Empire. Yeats called this (in the title phrase used for part of his *Autobiographies*) the "Tragic Generation", epitomising the fatalism of the period. Not surprisingly, then, the culture of the 1890s is rich with apocalyptic images. Take, for example, the description by two women writers (who published under the pseudonym "Michael Field") of their reaction on seeing the first volume of the notorious "Yellow Book" on display in a shop window in April, 1894:

> We have been almost blinded by the glare of hell... As we came up to the shop we found the whole frontage a hot background of orange-colour to sly, roistering heads, silhouetted against it and half-hiding behind masks... One hates one's eyes for seeing! But the infamous window mocked and mowed and fizgiged, saffron and pitchy, till one's eyes were arrested like Virgil's before the wind of flame. (Thornton 1970: 16)

This account may represent an almost hysterical response to decadence as embodied in the "Yellow Book", but what is particularly striking is that it is cast in terms of hell, judgement and apocalyptic destruction. It is surely significant, too, that in this facing up to "the glare of hell" the onlookers and would-be readers, whose eyes are "arrested" by the sight, become transformed into actors in a kind of theatre. Their heads are "silhouetted" against an unnatural "background" and they themselves are surrealistically "half-hiding behind masks" like the players in a stylised theatrical performance. The passage suggests a breakdown, not only of normal cultural and moral values, but also of the safe relationship between onlookers and actors. It is no longer certain who is watching whom, a feature of many of the plays from the 1890s and a particularly intriguing aspect of the popular genres of revue and music hall. The 'mirroring' function of theatre is suggested here in all its destabilising complexity.

Alongside the decadent and apocalyptic images of the 1890s already suggested here, I want to add another by means of a short poem by Arthur Symons which appeared in his collection *London Nights* (1895/7). As so often happens in lyric poems, the poignant brevity of the piece manages to contain within it a hint of the age in its "quintessence" (as Symons himself wrote), "fixing" a representative fragment of an era "fleetingly". The poem is particularly relevant to our considerations since it goes backstage in a theatre, suggesting the tattered reality behind the illusion of the stage. This is the first poem of a series called "Décor de Théâtre" and is individually entitled "Behind the Scenes — Empire" (a reference to the London Empire theatre). The mixture of ingredients in the poem's three levels of title — the geographical location "London Nights", the French term "Décor de Théâtre" and the grand theatrical name "Empire" — offers in miniature a reminder of the recipe of the 1890s: an urban culture, a consciously European artfulness, and fading imperial pride. Introduced by these pointers, the poem itself reads as follows:

> The little painted angels flit,
>   See, down the narrow staircase, where
> The pink legs flicker over it!
>
> Blonde, and bewigged, and winged with gold,
>   The shining creatures of the air
> Troop sadly, shivering with cold.
>
> The gusty gaslight shoots a thin
>   Sharp finger over cheeks and nose
>   Rouged to the colour of the rose.
>
> All wigs and paint, they hurry in:
>   Then, bid their radiant moment be
>   The footlights' immortality! (Thornton 1970: 42)

Like all glimpses backstage, the lyric highlights the incongruity of ordinariness and stage magic. The context is shoddy (a "narrow staircase", cold, lit only by "gusty gaslight") and the beauty is sadly artificial ("all wigs and paint"), yet there is an impression, an illusion perhaps, of the ethereal. These singing and dancing actresses are, briefly, "angels", with "pink legs" which "flicker" daintily; these "shining creatures of the air", "winged with gold", are "radiant", fuelled by a hope of fame, the "immortality" that the theatre "footlights" can achieve. This brittle lyric conveys much which is special to the 1890s, not just through the imagined smell of the gaslights, the strange fantasy of the popular music theatre, and the melancholic perception of how fragile artifice can be. The most significant feature, in my view, introducing a vital ingredient in the culture of the 1890s, is the fact that the "little painted angels" who fascinate the poet are undoubtedly female.

An obsession with the female in all her varied manifestations is one of the most dominant aspects of the 1890s. The final decade of the nineteenth century marks the meeting point of old and new in the definition of femininity. Much of the era's decadence in art and literature focussed on the female body in the centuries-old stereotype of the sexually voracious 'femme fatale', while at the same time this was the decade of the 'New Woman' in politics and society as well as in the plays of Ibsen and his contemporaries. (For a discussion of the 'New Woman' in British theatre of the 1890s, see the essay by Jean Chothia in this volume). Theatre and society were both substantially concerned with the changing politics of gender, an issue suggested even in the titles of plays such as Wilde's *Salome*, Sydney Grundy's *The New Woman*, Pinero's *The Notorious Mrs. Ebbsmith* and Jones's *The Case of Rebellious Susan*. As Elaine Showalter has importantly pointed out, psychology also played its part in putting gender on the agenda of the decade. Freud's *Studies on Hysteria* was published in 1895, while in France Dr. Jean-Martin Charcot experimented with female hysterics in a bizarre compromise between science and theatre (Showalter 1987: 147-154). With this public scientific contemplation of madness as the peculiarly 'female malady', the boundaries between medicine and psychoanalysis, and between role-play and self-expression, were blurred. In the late seventeenth century, when women first appeared on the English stage, they were seen as loose women, prostituting their bodies to be stared at in the theatre; in the 1890s, the science of psychiatry licensed a similar treatment of the female body as spectacle. The equation was therefore turned around — no longer the actress as whore, but the madwoman as actor. Among the most popular 'parts' which doctors urged women in lunatic asylums to 'play' was that of Ophelia; madwomen were photographed in an Ophelia pose for medical textbooks of the period (see Showalter 1987: 90-93). Thus when it came to women and madness, science copied the theatre, and the theatre mimicked science. However, when the actress Ellen Terry went to an asylum to get inspiration in her preparation for playing Ophelia, she commented ironically that the madwomen were "too *theatrical*" to be useful to her (Terry: 98).

So *Hamlet* returns to our discussion, with the ideas of theatre which we considered earlier now renewed and seen in gendered terms. It is no coincidence that *Hamlet* was a particularly popular play in the 1890s, on the public stage as well as in the asylums; a theatrical era is defined as much by what it chooses to revive as by what is written afresh. In *Hamlet*, the whole issue of gender construction is rendered uncertain. Through being associated with madness and acting, Hamlet himself is seen as feminine, forced to "unpack" his "heart with words" in the manner of "a whore" (2.2.538). The 1890s preoccupation with femininity and effeminacy represents, like so much else in the decade, a curiosity about the limits of the normal, and an unease with recognised social and cultural categories. What were the boundaries of gender difference, of theatrical illusion and reality, of decadence and morality, of old and new? Theatre in the 1890s was in large part an attempt to redefine those borders.

The mixture of darkness and levity, drama and decadence, which we discern in the mood of the 1890s is very much that of the last decade of a century. The 1590s, the decade in which *Hamlet* was engendered, was marked in England by triumphalism and melancholy in fairly even measure, while the 1690s witnessed the libertine despair of the Restoration sceptical vision and the 1790s saw a mingling of liberation and pessimism across Europe in the aftermath of the French Revolution. Conservatism is under threat in these eras, and yet clings on in the face of innovation. In England in the 1890s, for instance, there were cross-dressed productions of *Hamlet* which explored the stereotyping of gender and character, but in the same period this gender-bending was parodied in the many plays which appealed to more backward-looking ideological trends. There are, of course, two principles in opposition here: that art challenges and changes society, and that art reflects and follows the patterns set by society. Our deliberations in this volume may help to clarify which of these principles was the more dominant in the European theatre of 1894.

I shall conclude this introductory paper with another English poem from the 1890s, this one by Ernest Dowson from his *Verses* of 1896. As its subject is the brevity of life ("Vitae Summa Brevis Spem Nos Vetat Incohare Longam"), it is apt for the end of my brief thoughts on this era of endings:

> They are not long, the weeping and the laughter,
>   Love and desire and hate:
> I think they have no portion in us after
>   We pass the gate.
>
> They are not long, the days of wine and roses:
>   Out of a misty dream
> Our path emerges for a while, then closes
>   Within a dream. (Thornton: 228)

The "weeping and the laughter", Dowson's definition of living, would seem to hint at the elements of apocalypse and decadence which we have seen characterising the 1890s, as well as reminding us of the hysteria in the theatres and asylums of the decade. The reference to "desire", trapped between the more familiar opposites, love and hate, evokes the physical intensity of the era's culture and experience. But the poem also has a theatrical air, stirring some images not only of the "weeping and the laughter" which drama can draw out of us, but also of the "misty dream" of theatre itself, which Hamlet called a "dream of passion" (2.2.504). However, Shakespeare used the same dream metaphor when he likened human beings to actors: we are all "such stuff / As dreams are made on" (*The Tempest* 4.1.156-7), for our lives are the material of the theatrical dream. Is Dowson's poem, then, about living, or about living drama? Life, to Dowson, is a path which briefly "emerges" from a "misty dream" and later "closes" by returning to a dream. We often refer to theatre as a means of escape, a dream world mistily mirroring reality; here it is life which is an escape, a momentary release from the dream to which it eventually returns. The balance between living and acting, waking and dreaming, the life of the decade and its dramatic mirror, is, typically, unsettled here. We finish the poem in a state of creative uncertainty as to whether the "closing" of the life "within a dream" in the last line represents the closing or the opening of stage curtains in an 1890s theatre ...

References

Dowson, E., *Verses*. London, 1896.

Shakespeare, W., *Hamlet*, edited by Philip Edwards, Cambridge: Cambridge University Press, 1985.

Shakespeare, W., *The Tempest*, edited by Frank Kermode, London: Methuen, 1954.

Showalter, E., *The Female Malady: Women Madness and English Culture, 1830-1980*. London: Virago, 1987.

Symons, A., *London Nights*. London, 1897, 2nd. ed.

Terry, E., *The Story of My Life*. New York: Schocken, 1982.

Thornton, R.K.R. (ed.), *Poetry of the Nineties*. Harmondsworth: Penguin, 1970.

Jean Chothia
THE NEW WOMAN AND ENGLISH THEATRE IN 1894

The obsessive topic of 1890s English theatre is 'The Woman Question' in its various forms: female transgression of the moral or, even more, the social code; the anomalies of 'the double standard'; women's attempts at self-definition, and the threat their claims to education and emancipation pose to family, society and traditional perceptions of gender roles. Familiar in English fiction of the period and increasingly discussed in the press, these topics, feeding a seemingly insatiable demand, are addressed, satirically, tentatively, sympathetically, from the early 1890s onwards in play after play, and by all the leading dramatists of the time. They recur in the plays of fashionable West End theatres, crop up in farces and comic opera and inform the early attempts to establish alternative or independent theatres that follow the foundation of Antoine's Théâtre libre in Paris in 1887. And 1894 is notably the year of the new woman in English theatre. The very term, which seems to have appeared first in an article in May of that year[1], became widespread in September when Sidney Grundy satirized aspirations to female emancipation in his successful play, entitled, *The New Woman*, and *The Idler* devoted a whole issue to derision and denunciation of advanced women. An article surveying the scene in 1895 argued that the new drama had "brought the psychology of the feminine into glaring relief both in literature and on the stage so that the modern play and the modern novel are women's plays and women's novels, while the study of the masculine degenerates by comparison."[2]

Two European plays, Ibsen's *A Doll's House* produced at the Royalty by Janet Achurch and Charles Charrington in 1889 and Dumas fils's *Lady of the Camellias* toured by Duse in 1893 stimulated, fed and helped polarise this interest. The one was championed by the small body of socialists, feminists and others committed to a theatre of art rather than commerce; the other offered the glamour and sentiment that packed West End theatres and pleased businessmen on the look-out for saleable dramatic products that would fill their theatres for the minimum 50 nights that guaranteed profits.

Female emancipation was of course an issue before the *Doll's House* production but the slamming door of Nora's final exit, witnessed on the public stage and reverberating in newspaper columns, put the idea of a woman taking her fate into her own hands, clearly into the public domain. The play generated articles in the editorial as well as the theatre columns, and the emancipated woman with her claims to self-knowledge, education or financial independence became one of the regular butts of cartoons and humorous rhymes in that influential bastion of male humour and prejudice, *Punch*.

The themes of these foreign plays were variously resisted by and absorbed into the writing of Henry Arthur Jones and Arthur Wing Pinero, whose Society Dramas, which introduced excitingly novel material but retained the attitudes and structure of the French well-made play formula, with its exposition, complication, climax and revelatory denouement, quickly came to dominate the English stage in the 1890's retained too its prime interest in adultery and sexual danger. If Ibsen, as Shaw judged, did give "Victorian domestic morality its death-blow", Dumas fils offered it a momentary stay of execution. In a theatre that generated some 60 new plays a year the success of Jones and Pinero led popular writers such as Sidney Grundy and G.R. Sims to switch their attention to aspects of the woman question. It also prompted Oscar Wilde and Bernard Shaw, the two dramatists whose work has survived the period, to utilize their familiarity with the conventions for their own, rather different, comic and subversive ends.

The Lady of the Camellias, the quintessential nineteenth century play about female transgression had played throughout Europe following its first appearance in 1852. Forbidden by the English censor, however, it only reached the London stage some 40 years later. Its courtesan heroine, Marguerite Gautier, persuaded by the father of the man she truly loves to renounce him rather than compromise his social position, deserts him. The touching final scene, in which the young man returns to find her dying of consumption and, at last, recognises the greatness of her love, allows the audience to weep for her self-sacrifice and her lover's remorse, safe in the knowledge that, since the transgressor is now sadly but safely dead, any threat to the moral code has been averted. Unsubversive, for all it allows titillating insight into the glamorous and, for the English middle classes, forbidden, world of the high class courtesan, it is a splendid male fantasy, flattering those who weep for the admittedly fallen but remorseful and generous-spirited woman prepared to sacrifice even the good opinion of the man she loves, for the good of the man himself. It spawned a host of woman-with-a-past imitations in the early 1890s whose success with audiences suggests that they chimed in with contemporary sentiment and anxiety. Most commonly, as in *The Second Mrs Tanqueray,* the play that, later in 1893, confirmed Pinero as the leading English dramatist, a woman who has erred sexually sacrifices herself for the man she loves and to redeem herself in the eyes of her — or his — innocent daughter. (Men in these plays — particularly the *raisonneurs,* the plays' invariably male authority figures — are frequently acknowledged to have had mistresses. Much of the verbal spark comes from the raciness of the talk of these worldly rationalizers so that, even where the plot seems to indite the double standard, the texture of the dialogue endorses it.)

The Second Mrs Tanqueray was thought particularly advanced because the husband in it knew of his wife's past when he married her. Paula realises that when sexual attraction has gone there will be nothing — precisely the argument which vanquished Marguerite Gautier. At the end of Pinero's play, Paula says, simply, "I'm sorry, Aubrey", and goes to an off-stage suicide. Henry James found the decision to allow Paula to die, "momentous" because it defied the rule of the happy ending.[3] Bernard Shaw, coiner of the term 'Pineroticism' as a riposte to *Punch'* s 'Ibsenity', more alert to the pattern, scornfully denounced the heroine's unresisting self-sacrifice to the dominant moral ethos, her remorse for her deplorable past and her inability any longer to look a 'good woman', in the face.[4]

Oscar Wilde became a gleeful practitioner of the form in the years immediately surrounding 1894. In *Lady Windermere's Fan* (1892); *A Woman of No Importance* (1893) and *An Ideal Husband* (1895) the familiar patterns are both relished and exposed; audience expectations, flattered and mocked. Consider Wilde's plots and devices: a fallen woman tries to get back; she infiltrates the company of the daughter who has idealised her memory, a letter is intercepted; a mislaid fan threatens to destroy a reputation; a chance encounter reveals paternity; a betrayed woman, insulted by her former lover, strikes him with her glove; an overheard conversation effects a change of heart; ancient shady financial deals return to haunt a man on the brink of a brilliant political career; a blackmailer is foiled. The lessons of the French well-made play have been well absorbed.

The current of feeling in *Lady Windermere's Fan*, for example, as well as its jokes, undercut the sanctity of the social law. The audience is drawn to laugh *with* the sinful mother, Mrs. Erlynne, who mocks the very genre in which she finds herself. She forces recognition of its artificiality, when she refuses to "...weep on her neck and tell her who I am, all that kind of thing" or to "retire to a convent or become a hospital nurse or something of that kind as people do in silly modern novels." (Act IV) Wilde's closest model, Pierre Leclerq's *Illusion*, ended with the penitent fallen woman returning dressed in widow's weeds.[5] Mrs Erlynne, by contrast, ensnares the wealthy Lord Augustus and observes that, "if a woman really repents, she has to go to a bad dressmaker, otherwise no-one believes in her. And nothing in the world would induce me to do that." But for all the parody Wilde's play is fundamentally reassuring. Mrs Erlynne follows conventional wisdom in ensuring her errant daughter returns to her marriage and not only is Lord Augustus an evidently silly man but it is clear they will have to leave the country to enjoy their wealth.

Unlike the Dumas fils play that was widely praised, Ibsen's provoked anger and fierce partisan support. It generated a different order of discussion because it asked awkward questions about every woman's role in contemporary society. The audience of *A Doll's House* does not look vicariously into a different world. Instead of a glamorous courtesan, the play puts a middle class housewife on the stage (the words 'suburban' and 'dowdy' recur in reviews) and is concerned not with courtship or adultery, but with the deceptions on which the seeming happiness of a marriage is founded and with the woman's growing perception that she has been her father's then her husband's doll with no identity of her own. It shows individuals struggling in a mesh formed by the economic structure of society and the habitual pattern of normal social interactions. Interrogating family structure directly, Ibsen shifts attention to the problematic nature of the marriage relationship in a world in which women without independent means are essentially kept by men for the services they provide. In other words, the play directly challenges current gender and power relations. In doing so it makes a claim for the theatre as a place where important questions of self and society are addressed. The opposition insisted it was a place for relaxation and light entertainment.

Particularly after Elizabeth Robins' powerful 1891 production added consciousness of *Hedda Gabler*, a peculiarly English echo of Ibsen is found in West End plays whose action daringly shows married women asserting themselves. Invariably, though, they are tempted not by Nora's need for self-discovery but, giving the audience the frisson of forbidden pleasure, by the love of a kinder man than their husband and their endings firmly repudiate Nora's choice by asserting overriding duty to husband and children, however oppressive the circumstances, and there are further excitements to be got from depiction of the circumstances. Two of Henry Arthur Jones's most celebrated plays on this theme appeared in 1894. In one, *The Masqueraders*, the plea to the generous-hearted admirer of the miserably married woman is expressed in terms of her duty to her children. "Keep her pure for her child":

> Save her to be a good mother to that little helpless creature she has brought into the world, so that when her girl grows up and she has to guide her, she'll not have to say to her child: "You can give yourself to this man, and if you don't like him you can give yourself to another, and to another, and so on. It doesn't matter." It was what I did.
>
> (Act IV)

so she is persuaded to stay with the husband who gambles, drinks and, it is implied, beats her, while after a sentimental parting, the lover leaves for probable death in darkest Africa.

The implication of Jones's other 1894 play, *The Case of Rebellious Susan*, is that the sin resides less in the doing than in the being found out. The play is fascinating both for what it seems to attempt and for the triviality of its finished form. The material for a fierce parody of Society Drama is here but is dissipated. The heroine, furious at the discovery of her husband's philandering although warned of possible consequences by the play's *raisonneur* and advised by one woman friend to nag for a fortnight and then forget it and by another to be 'mutely reproachful', look a little paler and wear prettier frocks, nevertheless does assert herself and at the end of Act I defiantly leaves to join a woman friend on a trip to Egypt. Returned in Act II, it is evident that, while abroad, she has formed a close relationship with another man. In Act III, the interest of the play shifts from the woman's dilemma to frantic defence of her reputation by friends who recognise that if scandal attaches to her, her husband cannot take her back. The play is resolved with a reconciliation and the husband's offer to buy his wife the biggest jewel he can find. The audience, who customarily applauded statements of principle they approved, evidently approved this enthusiastically.

This play's history, incidentally gives us an insight into the social context and power structures of the contemporary English theatre and the constraints on the writer who wanted his work performed. Charles Wyndham, the actor manager, claiming he was "simply voicing the public instinct", accepted the play on condition that cuts blurred the suggestion that Susan had repaid the adultery in kind and expressed astonishment that Jones should imagine that he could "induce married men to bring their wives to the theatre to learn the lesson that they can descend to such nastiness as giving themselves up for an evening of adulterous pleasure and then return safely to their husband's arms, provided they are clever enough, low enough, and dishonest enough to avoid being found out."[6] Jones acquiesced, removing words that made it clear Susan had slept with her admirer, and claiming, "I would not willingly offend any single person among my audience; indeed, I would at some violence to my own convictions, remove any scene that would hurt the natural reverence of any spectator."[7] [British theatre had won its way to respectability in the second half of the nineteenth century. The middle classes attended, wore evening dress in the stalls and wives did indeed go too. Henry Irving would be knighted by Queen Victoria in 1895 and the other leading actor managers would earn their knighthoods in the course of the decade, including Wyndham in 1897].

Jones's first attempt at English Ibsenism had notoriously involved a more extreme adjustment to current taste. His *Breaking a Butterfly* in 1884 was a version of *A Doll's House*, with its leading characters anglicised as Humphrey and Flora. Granville Barker wrote of the ending:

> Burlesque could do no more. Torvald-Humphrey behaves like the pasteboard hero of Nora's old doll's house dream: he does strike his chest and say: "I am the guilty one." And Nora-Flora cries out that she is a poor weak foolish girl "no wife for a man like you. You are a thousand times too good for me" and never wakes up and walks out of her doll's house at all.[8]

A Doll's House marked the definitive arrival into English consciousness of the emancipated woman. Indeed, emancipated women appeared immediately afterwards in Pinero's *The Weaker Sex* (1889) and Jones's *Judah* (1890). Among the vicious abuse that Ibsen's plays habitually stimulated is a particular strain of attack that reiterates the threat to English domestic life of the perceived message of emancipation and singles out women admirers. So, *Queen* warned that, "the result of preaching the doctrine that every woman ought to emancipate herself" will be "a dangerous general rebellion of women" and Clement Scott, the leading English theatre critic of the day, or at least the leader of 'the Ancients' where William Archer led 'the Moderns', argued that the play promoted a 'new creed' in which the ideal of woman was no longer a "fountain of love and forgiveness and charity, the pattern woman we have admired in our mothers and sisters", but "a mass of aggregate conceit and self-sufficiency, who", and this is the real horror which the heroine of Jones's

Masqueraders would reject, "leaves her home and deserts her friendless children because she has *herself* to look after."[9] The unnaturalness of all this spills over onto the Ibsen audience who are observed as, "de-sexed...the socialist and the sexless...the unwomanly, the unsexed females, the whole army of unprepossessing cranks in petticoats...effeminate man and male women", and, attending the premiere of *Ghosts* in 1891:

> ordinary commonplace women and girls that had come out of mere prurient curiosity were mixed up with spectacled, green complex-ioned, oddly dressed females of unhealthy aspect, their bodies seemingly as diseased as their minds.

The danger to society through contagion of the weaker vessels by the freaks becomes apparent. The ordinary women at first were embarrassed:

> But, observing that the spectacled and green complexioned of their sex devoured the dirty morsels with such relish that can only be com-pared to that of a dog who has found some uncommonly tasty tit-bit in a gutter, they soon shook off their silly conventional modesty, which is only a fashion deep, and seemed to enjoy them as well as the emancipated.[10]

Although the woman figured on the poster for Grundy's *The New Woman* is yellow- rather than green-complexioned her kind is instantly recognisable by the contemporary signifiers of threat and absurdity. Her books, with their feminist titles are scattered untidily on the floor, onto which an unsorted pile of papers spills — she is clearly no housewife; unchaperoned, she has her own door key hanging on the wall; in a period in which, following Wyndham's 1889 coup of dressing his actresses in gowns designed by Worth, theatre managers vied with each other to put their leading ladies in the most glamorous outfits, her dress is plain, her hair unkempt and, of course, she wears spectacles. What is more, as the cigarette at the edge of the poster reveals, not only does she smoke but does so ignorantly: this has clearly first been lit at the wrong end. The poster only lacks a bicycle which, with tobacco and rational dress, was ubiquitous in contemporary images of female self-sufficiency.

Grundy satirizes the very idea of female emancipation. His feminists bicker about whether women should be allowed to be as sinful as men or men made to be as virtuous as women. His older male characters, comment with unreconstructed lasciviousness on the young women's figures and faces and mock the aspiration to education and equality of Mrs Sylvester, the emancipated women of the title. The feminist books on the shelves are derided with heavy-footed jokes that might have come straight from the pages of *Punch*.

COLONEL (reads): "Man the Betrayer" by Edith Bethune.
SYLVESTER: Oh I know her. She comes to our house.
COLONEL: And has a man betrayed her?
SYLVESTER: Never. Not likely to.
COLONEL: That's what's the matter perhaps — "Naked and Un-
ashamed — a Few Plain Facts and Figures." Mary Bevan M.D. Who on
earth's she?
SYLVESTER: One of the plain figures. (Act I)

A minor character, Elaine, in *The Case of Rebellious Susan*, is described in
Jones's stage directions as, *"a raw, assertive, modern young lady, with brusque
and decided manner."* She is mockingly challenged by the play's *raisonneur*
who, representing the commonsense viewpoint, rehearses a famous question:
"What is it that you ladies want? You are evidently dissatisfied with being
a woman. You cannot wish to be anything so brutal and disgusting as a man
and unfortunately there is no neuter sex in the human species. What do you
want?" (Act III)
Discontented, disrupting the status quo, such characters are also represented
as neurotic and sexually perverse. They are either frigid or possessed by
voracious sexual appetite, sometimes bizarrely, both together. Grundy's Mrs
Sylvester, cold towards her husband, pretends to a relationship of the mind
with the hero, Gerald, but is in reality set on sexual seduction. Although
much more sympathetically portrayed, Agnes Ebbsmith, the free-thinking
heroine of Pinero's *The Notorious Mrs Ebbsmith*, (1895) reveals her dubious
sexuality in her horror of passion and her proposal to Lucas that they live
platonically but, when she perceives that she may lose him, she recognises
that she is a weak woman after all and resorts to age-old feminine wiles,
replacing her plain dress with the glamorous, decolleté evening gown Lucas
has brought. She recognises that she must be one thing or the other: "I was
to lead women...but the figure was made of wax — it fell away at the first hot
breath that touched it." (Act IV) Although Lucas is indited for moral
weakness, it is his viewpoint that the play endorses when to Agnes's cry, "I
believe to be a woman is to be mad" he replies, "No, to be a woman trying
not to be a woman, that is to be mad." (Act III)
More sympathetically conceived emancipated women such as Agnes discover
their true selves in the course of the action. Lucas cries joyfully, "You really
love me, you mean — as simple, tender women are content to love" (Act V);
indeterminate or sexually voracious freaks are defeated by womanly women
such as Margery in Grundy's play who declares herself simply what God
made her — a woman; "take love away from us" she appeals to her feminist
rival, "and you take life itself. You have your books, your sciences, your
brains. What have we? — nothing but our broken hearts" (Act III), and her
self-abnegating devotion wins the day.
Agnes Ebbsmith's lover is "a highly strung emotional creature" and Agnes
can "hear his nerves vibrating". Although Jones's character declared "there is
no neuter sex", the men who sympathise with women's emancipation are

portrayed as effeminate and given silly names to match. Elaine's admirer, Fergusson Pybus, is effete, aesthetically dressed and with mincing speech. A hanger-on in *The New Women* is called Percy Pettigrew and the feminisation of Gerald is signalled visually in the opening stage direction of his room which is "*somewhat effeminately decorated. The furniture of the boudoir type, several antimacassars and a profusion of photographs and flowers*", while his uncle says explicitly, "these people are a sex of their own. They have invented a new gender. And to think my nephew's one of them." (Act I) Oscar Wilde, writing *The Importance of Being Earnest* in the autumn of 1894, is unabashed. The dress, hairstyle and beautifully furnished rooms of Algernon Moncrieff (typical *Punch* name) signal that he is certainly an aesthete. Neither mincing nor effete, he is also a man of sharp wit and vigorous life. The self-possession of Gwendolen and Cecily similarly mark them as modern young women of decided opinions. Unlike the caricatured new women they are allowed to understand the implications of what is said and, doing so, to make telling thrusts. To Miss Prism's "I suppose you know where socialism leads?" Cecily replies, "Oh yes! that leads to rational dress, Miss Prism. And I suppose when a women is dressed rationally, she is treated rationally" while Gwendolen, needing cover for her jaunt, claims an unusually long lecture at the University Extension Scheme.

But Wilde's capacity to combine such ideas with socially and theatrically acceptable plays was rare. Besides the actor managers alert to the attitudes of their audiences, an active censorship stood ready to defend. If Henry Arthur Jones would not willingly have offended a single member of his audience, the Lord Chamberlain's Chief Examiner of Plays, E.F. Smythe Piggott, with the power to cut or ban on religious, political or moral grounds, was on hand to make sure that no-one else did either. Shaw labelled him "a walking compendium of vulgar prejudice"[11], but he was specifically chosen not to lead but to represent mainstream taste. The gross generalizations of his testimony to the Parliamentary Select Committee to enquire into censorship in 1892, demonstrates how thoroughly he did so:

> Ibsen's plays appear to me morally deranged. All the heroines are dissatisfied spinsters who (...) look on marriage as a monopoly, or dissatisfied married women in a chronic state of rebellion against not only the conditions which nature has imposed on their sex, but against all the duties and obligations of mothers and wives; as for men, they are all rascals and imbeciles.[12]

When the Anglo-Dutchman, Jacob Grein, financed by a £50 cheque from the Dutch Theatre managers for introducing them to the works of Pinero and Jones, opened the English Independent Theatre with a closed house performance of *Ghosts*, the next day's papers, morally outraged by the references to syphilis and to the seeming endorsement of Mrs Alving's proposed adultery, demanded closure of the loophole that enabled a subscription club to avoid censorship.[13] The chief works of the European avant garde theatres, Tolstoi's *Power of Darkness*; Ibsen's *Ghosts* and Hauptmann's *The Weavers* were all banned from the English stage — *Ghosts* was finally licensed in 1914 and Grein only got his licence to produce Tolstoi's play in 1931, 40 years after he first applied for it. Wilde's *Salome* was banned before it could be performed in 1892 (Wilde's very name would be removed from posters for *The Importance of Being Earnest* after his arrest for gross indecency in 1895 and the professional theatre would close ranks against him on his conviction, none of his plays being seen again in England until the new century) and Shaw's *Mrs Warren's Profession* written in 1893, had its first public performance not in 1894 but in 1925.

Instead of a female transgressor sighing over the past, Shaw sets Mrs Warren, a vulgar, middle aged business woman, with brothels in every European city, against her daughter, Vivie, a freethinking, new woman but one initially as innocent as Ellean Tanqueray of her mother's past and profession. Shaw develops the caricature with gusto: gives Vivie Warren a strong handshake, a propensity for rational dress and cigars and a charming but weak idler as lover. (With humorous reference to Philippa Fawcett, who startled the Academic world in 1890 by coming out above the top male student in the Cambridge mathematics tripos). Vivie has settled for the next to the top place in order not to have had to over exert herself. Mrs Warren is robust in her own defence: there is no sighing over lost innocence. Her rejection of honourable poverty, marriage to a laborer or menial work interrogates assumptions in the language:

> What sort of a woman do you take me for? How could you keep your self-respect in such starvation and slavery? And what's a woman worth? What's a life worth? without self respect. Why am I independent and able to give my daughter a first rate education when other women that had just as good opportunities are in the gutter? Because I always knew how to respect myself and control myself... Don't you be led away by people who don't know the world, my girl. The only way for a woman to provide for herself decently is for her to be good to some man that can afford to be good to her.

Prostitution in Mrs Warren's eyes is the least damaging of the alternatives available. Like the French Naturalists, Shaw focuses on the larger economics of prostitution, seeing it as a trade in human beings, an integral part of capitalism and the free market. In the course of the play, the audience is educated with Vivie in economic reality, is asked to see the complicity of everyone in the wrongs of the economic and social system. Vivie's personal crisis is of a different kind from Ellean Tanqueray's. Recognising the terrifying absurdity of the situation she neither learns retrospective generosity nor yields to male authority, although the play dangles both options. Rejecting the demands both of her mother and of sexual relationship, she turns to her work. Just as the play has been a consciously distorted echo of

Society drama, so the final stage direction includes a conscious tribute to *A Doll's House*,

> Mrs Warren goes out, slamming the door behind her. The strain on Vivie's face relaxes; her grave expression breaks up into one of joyous content

and she settles down to work. We are left with disturbing questions about the relationship between such rejections and the capacity to live. The paradoxical recognition remains that Vivie is only who and how she is because Mrs Warren made money. She can give up the money but not her educated mind and social values, nor would she want to. It is crucial to Shaw's challenge to the audience that there is no catharsis. The good are inevitably compromised. We are not let off the hook; nor are the conventionally bad punished in any material way. Mrs Warren, a representative of a society in which the self-serving flourish, continues "to be prosperously immoral to the end of the play." It is fiercely polemical work. How could the censor not have forbidden it?

What of the real new women? To give this piece a happy ending, I ought to be able to produce some powerful plays by women with sympathetic advanced women characters to match the glut of New Woman novels in the same period.[14] It cannot be done — at least not until 1907 when Elizabeth Robins' *Votes for Women* heralds a flowering of such writing, now again becoming available.[15] But the ground *was* being prepared in the early 1890s. Whereas novelists need only to find a willing publisher, dramatists need a theatre, actors, technicians and an audience. One of the few, *Alan's Wife*, by Elizabeth Robins and Florence Bell produced anonymously by the Independent Theatre had proved too strong even for that audience and so became, like *Mrs Warren's Profession*, one of the plays not given public performance in 1894 and, indeed, essentially vanished until very recently. With its infant euthanasia it certainly would not have passed the censor. Ironically, given the furious assault on Robins' play, *The Spectator* reviewer wrote in response to her novel, *George Mandeville's Husband* published in 1894 under the pseudonym C.E. Raimond, "*he*, certainly understands women's distinctive graciousness and ungraciousness as few women of the advanced type appear to understand it."[16]

It is, I think, a symptomatic and shaping difference that, whereas Ibsen was introduced to French audiences via *Ghosts*, and the agency of the Théâtre libre, an evidently male-dominated organisation, led by Antoine's driven performance as Osvald, in England *A Doll's House* was the initiatory play and its production was driven by the passionate belief of its Nora, Janet Achurch, and when *Ghosts* was produced in 1891 English reviewers attended more censoriously to Mrs Alving's role. That it was actresses who kept up the pressure for Ibsen in England and that women were a notable part of the minority audience for avant garde drama marks a resistance to the extreme English conservatism that would marginalize them. Elizabeth Robins claimed that it was the hopelessly limited and unreal roles in mainstream theatre that initially fired her enthusiasm for Ibsen. Having been a powerful Hedda Gabler in her co-production with Marion Lea; Hilde Wangel and co-translator of *The Master Builder*; Mrs Linden in the *Doll's House* revival, 1894 found her taking Ibsen to the provinces with a season at the Manchester Independent Theatre. In 1896 Pinero's Paula Tanqueray, Stella Campbell, who claimed that playing Agnes Ebbsmith's renunciation "broke her heart" and who indeed seems to have played the later scenes with simmering anger against the grain of the play[17], would accept the role of the Rat Wife in *Little Eyolf* with Elizabeth Robins and Janet Achurch.

The English independent theatre movement was hesitant, lacking a director with the stage sense of an Antoine or a Lugné Poe[18] and choked by the strictures of the censor and the conservatism of the main stream managers and theatre goers. But the publication of such seemingly unperformable plays as Shaw and Robins had been stimulated to write for the avant garde theatre, as well as Ibsen's work and the widespread discussion they generated, helped stir up some at least of the theatre profession and create a more receptive audience in the next generation when, more than a decade after comparable events in Europe, the English New Drama would flourish and the Actress's Franchise League would be in the forefront of the suffrage movement.

One event in 1894, hardly noticed at the time, was prophetic of three separate strands of things to come. Florence Farr, another determined actress, who had initiated the English premiere of *Rosmersholm*, presented a double bill at the Avenue Theatre, financed by an anonymous benefactor. The plays were Yeats's mystical Irish play, *The Land of Heart's Desire* and Shaw's satirical comedy, *Arms and the Man*, with Alma Murray, Grundy's frightful Mrs Sylvester, appearing as Raina. Shaw's work would be the basis of the renewal of English theatre that came after the turn of the century, through the Stage Society and the Court Theatre; Yeats would, with Augusta Gregory, found the Irish Players at the turn of the century, through whose auspices first John Synge and then Sean O'Casey would find an audience for their work. Florence Farr's anonymous benefactor was another real new woman, Annie Horniman, who would subsequently fund the Abbey Theatre in Dublin for Yeats and through the Manchester Repertory Company would discover writers and an audience beyond London for the New English Drama.

Notes

1. Sarah Grand, 'The New Aspect of the Woman Question', in: *The North American Review* 158 (May, 1894).

2. 'The New Drama', unattributed, *The Quarterly Review* 182 (1895), 399-428: p. 411. See, too, 'The Fiction of Sexuality', *Contemporary Review* (April, 1895) for a parallel discussion of prose fiction.

3. James to Pinero, 2.5.93, quoted in ed L.Edel, *The Complete Plays of Henry James* (New York, 1949), p. 455.

4. Shaw, February 1895, reprinted in *Dramatic Opinion and Essays* vol. 1 (New York, 1907), p. 39.

5. For detailed discussion of Wilde's sources see Kerry Powell, *Oscar Wilde and the Theatre of the 1890s* (Cambridge, 1990), pp. 122-6.

6. Penny Griffin, *A.W. Pinero and H.A. Jones* (London, 1991), p. 37.

7. H.A. Jones, *The Renascence of the English Drama* (London, 1895), p. 50.

8. Barker in ed. Walter de la Mare, *The Eighteen Eighties* (Cambridge, 1930), p. 168.

9. *Queen* (15.6.89), quoted ed. M. Egan, *Ibsen, The Critical Heritage* (London, 1972), p. 106; 'the Ancients', so labelled in W.A. Bettany, *The Theatre* (June, 1892); and see James Woodfield, *The English Theatre in Transition* (London, 1984) pp. 16ff, for discussion of polarization among critics; Clement Scott, July 1889, *Critical Heritage*, p. 114.

10. *Truth*, quoted William Archer, *Pall Mall Gazette* (8.4.91), p. 3; *Licensed Victuallers' Mirror* (1.3.91), *Critical Heritage*, p. 202; 203.

11. Woodfield, p. 113.

12. S. Hynes, *The Edwardian Turn of Mind* (London, 1968), pp. 308-9.

13. For example: *Daily Telegraph; Daily Times; Evening News* and *Post*, all 14.3.91.

14. For example: Sarah Grand, *The Heavenly Twins* (London, 1893); George Egerton (Mary Dunne) *Keynotes* (London, 1893); George Egerton, *Discords* (London, 1894); Grant Allen, *The Woman Who Did* (London, 1895).

15. See e.g., ed. Spender and Hayman, *How the Vote Was Won and other Suffragette Plays* (London, 1985) and L. Fitzsimmons and V. Gardner, *New Woman Plays* (London, 1991).

16. Quotation reproduced as advertisement on back cover, Pinero, *The Notorious Mrs Ebbsmith* (London, 1895).

17. Persuasively argued by Joel Kaplan, 'Pineroticism and the Problem Play', ed. R. Foulkes, *British Theatre in the 1890s* (Cambridge, 1992), pp. 55-7.

18. See John Stokes' discussion of this in *Resistible Theatres* (London, 1972), p. 125.

A selection of cartoons from *Punch, or the London Charivari* (1894).

Donna Quixote.

'A world of disorderly notions *picked out of books*, crowded into his (her) imagination.' —*Don Quixote*

A 'New Woman.'

The Vicar's Wife. 'And have you had good sport, Miss Goldenberg?'
Miss. G. 'Oh, rippin'! I only shot one rabbit, but I managed to injure quite a dozen more!'

A LADIES' PARLIAMENT.

Henri Behar
ALFRED JARRY ET LE THÉÂTRE FRANÇAIS
À LA FIN DU XIXe SIÈCLE

Plus que pour toute autre rétrospective historique, parler du théâtre français il y a cent ans, c'est vous inviter à un *Voyage au pays de la quatrième dimension*, pour reprendre le titre d'un ouvrage d'un ami de Jarry, Gaston de Pawlovski, que le premier aurait fort goûté, tant il aimait se mouvoir dans ces univers imaginaires, s'il n'était mort avant sa publication, en 1912.

En effet, aux trois dimensions de l'espace auxquelles nous sommes habitués, il faut en ajouter une autre, la temporelle, qui, elle-même, se décompose en plusieurs séquences:

— Il y a la chronologie (apparemment) toute simple de l'histoire littéraire, fondée sur les principaux faits et les dates de publication des ouvrages, dont on ne retiendra que ceux qui sont en relation avec le théâtre.

— Puis, il y a le temps de la représentation, celui des reprises permanentes d'oeuvres à succès, et celui des créations, parfois pour une ou deux soirées seulement, des 'théâtres à côté', comme on disait alors, à quoi Adolphe Aderer consacrait quelques articles, tandis que Francisque Sarcey occupait, avec son important feuilleton, le rez de chaussée du journal *Le Temps*.[1] Il ne faut pas oublier que la pièce de Musset, *Lorenzaccio*, que nous considérons aujourd'hui comme le principal drame romantique, ne fut montée sur la scène de la Renaissance, avec Sarah Bernhardt dans le rôle titre, qu'en décembre 1896!

— Ces deux durées, quoique d'essence différente, sont encore facilement conciliables. Mais il faut y ajouter la question du point de vue: doit-on, se plaçant délibérément à l'époque de référence, considérer les spectacles en fonction de leur succès, de l'événement public qu'ils ont alors constitué, ou bien, usant du filtre de l'histoire, ne retenir que ce qui, à nos yeux de lecteurs et surtout de spectateurs d'aujourd'hui compte encore? Si je me réfère à un ouvrage sur le théâtre contemporain publié 'à chaud', en 1898, voici les tendances et les auteurs auxquels il consacre un chapitre: Dumas fils, Emile Augier, Edouard Pailleron, Henry Becque; le Théâtre-Libre; la Comédie nouvelle: Jules Lemaître, Eugène Brieux, Henri Lavedan, Paul Hervieu, Maurice Donnay; Renaissance du vers dramatique: Jean Richepin, Edmond Rostand.[2] Vous m'accorderez que ce n'est pas exactement le palmarès retenu aujourd'hui!

On le voit, ces problèmes de temporalité et de sélection ne peuvent être résolus d'un trait de plume. Comme notre planète, j'aurais tendance à dire que l'histoire du théâtre, il y a cent ans, est faite de creux et de bosses.

Pour évoquer l'année théâtrale 1894, il est donc nécessaire de se reporter quelques années en arrière, à l'époque où André Antoine fonde le Théâtre libre, et peut-être antérieurement, quand la Comédie-Française recevait (fort mal) *Les Corbeaux* de Becque, en élargissant l'éventail au moins jusqu'à la représentation d'*Ubu roi*, par Lugné-Poe à l'Oeuvre.

Pour fixer les idées, j'établirai une brève chronologie, tenant compte des divers paramètres auxquels je viens de faire référence, m'en tenant, pour l'essentiel, aux oeuvres dramatiques et aux faits littéraires s'y rapportant d'une certaine manière.

1881 — Zola: *Le Naturalisme au théâtre*.

1882 — Becque: *Les Corbeaux* (Comédie Française, même année).

1885 — Jean Moréas: 'Manifeste du symbolisme', *Figaro*, 18 sept. Becque: *La Parisienne*.

1887-1897 — Antoine anime le Théâtre libre.

1887 — Maupassant, Rosny, Guiches, Bonnetain, P. Marguerite se rebellent contre *La Terre* de Zola et publient leur 'Manifeste des cinq'.

1889 — création de *La Revue blanche*. Maeterlinck: *La Princesse Maleine* (Théâtre d'Art, 1890).

1890-1892 — Paul Fort anime le Théâtre d'Art.

1890 — Fondation du *Mercure de France*. Villiers de l'Isle-Adam: *Axel* (Théâtre de la rive gauche, février 1894). Claudel: *Tête d'or* (première version).

1891 — Enquête de Jules Huret sur l'évolution littéraire. 'Naturalisme pas mort', câble Paul Alexis. Jamais à court d'invention, Jean Moréas lance l'Ecole romane. Immense succès d'*Amoureuse* de Porto-Riche (publié en 1894).

1892 — Maeterlinck *Pelléas et Mélisande* (Théâtre de l'Oeuvre, 1893).

1893 — Lugné-Poe fonde le Théâtre de l'Oeuvre.

1894 — Le capitaine Dreyfus est condamné. Verlaine est élu Prince des poètes. Feydeau: *Un fil à la patte* (Palais-Royal). Renard: *Poil de carotte* (Théâtre Antoine, 1900).

1895 — à Bussang, Maurice Pottecher fonde le Théâtre du peuple. Tristan Bernard: *Les Pieds nickelés* (Théâtre de l'Oeuvre).

1896 — Mallarmé est à son tour élu Prince des poètes. Jules Renard: *La Demande*. Jarry: *Ubu roi* (Théâtre de l'Oeuvre). Feydeau: *Monsieur chasse; Le Dindon*.

1897 — Saint-Georges Bouhélier fonde le Naturisme. Péguy: *Jeanne d'Arc*. Renard: *Le Plaisir de rompre*.

1898 — Zola entre dans la mêlée de l'Affaire Dreyfus avec son pamphlet 'J'accuse', publié par *L'Aurore*. L'épilogue en sera la réhabilitation du capitaine en 1906. Rostand: *Cyrano de Bergerac*.

1899 — Saint-Pol Roux: *La Dame à la faulx*. Feydeau: *La dame de chez Maxim*.

1900 — Courteline: *Le Commissaire est bon enfant*. Rostand: *L'Aiglon* (Théâtre Sara-Bernhardt).

1901 — Le premier prix Nobel de littérature est attribué à Sully Prudhomme.

Sur le plan de l'histoire du théâtre, cette période a été abondamment explorée, tant pour ce qui concerne le texte que pour la scénographie. Par souci pédagogique, pour des raisons de clarté aussi, les manuels ont coutume de consacrer un chapitre au Théâtre Libre d'Antoine, considéré comme le père-fondateur de la mise en scène, puis un autre à l'Oeuvre de Lugné-Poe, présenté comme son principal opposant; Paul Fort, avec son Théâtre d'Art, étant tenu pour l'amateur préfigurant ce qu'on a appelé, un peu schématiquement, *La Réaction idéaliste au théâtre*.[3] Plutôt que de me référer à des essais anciens, dont les vues sont toujours excitantes pour l'esprit, tels ceux d'Albert Thibaudet ou d'Henri Clouard, ou mieux encore à des histoires du spectacle et du théâtre en France, élaborées par des érudits austères, j'en prendrai pour témoin le dernier ouvrage en date, une fort originale *Histoire du théâtre dessinée*, publiée en 1992 par un amateur passionné, André Degaine.[4] Dans la section intitulée 'Le temps des metteurs en scène', se succèdent les chapitres consacrés à Antoine et à Lugné-Poe. En dépit de sa nécessaire brièveté et d'un souci de vulgarisation contraignant à l'essentiel, l'information en est très sûre. Tout en vous invitant à vous y reporter, ne serait-ce que pour l'illustration, irremplaçable, je me permettrai d'en citer plusieurs extraits, qui situent bien notre problème.

> Techniques du Théâtre Libre:
> — on joue comme s'il n'y avait pas de spectateurs. Parfois **de dos**. Très nouveau à une époque où les bas de pantalons étaient roussis par les becs de gaz de la rampe, à force de jeu 'au public'.
> — on soigne le mouvement des scènes **d'ensemble**. Antoine va voir, en Belgique, les mises en scène des 'Meiningen' qu'il admire.
> — on préconise, pour le travail du comédien, l'observation, l'étude **directe** de la nature. Antoine s'en réfère à Molière: 'jouer comme l'on parle'. Il raille le ton 'théâtral' des acteurs hors scène.
> — le rideau de scène devient le '**4ème mur**' qui se lève sur tel intérieur minutieusement reconstitué. Le spectateur assiste, par effraction, à une '**tranche de vie**'. Rejet de la 'pièce bien faite' avec des scènes 'à faire', intrigue bien ficelée, personnage du 'raisonneur', idylle amoureuse obligée. Goût du 'spectacle coupé' (suite de courtes pièces) expérimental.
> — par pauvreté, à ses débuts, Antoine utilise des **meubles véritables** (prêtés par les parents et les amis) et même des **quartiers de viande** (empruntés au boucher voisin) pour *Les Bouchers* (1888). Leur odeur incommode même certains spectateurs.
> — les costumes viennent du **fripier**, non du loueur.
> — on tâche de **convertir** au théâtre les grands écrivains, d'abolir la "funeste dissociation (...) entre le théâtre et la littérature". (Edmond Sée)
> '**La reproduction de la réalité** par les moyens mêmes de la réalité' s'impose, sur le moment, comme une évidence. La critique et les amateurs de théâtre saluent Antoine comme un novateur incontournable. L'Europe entière suit![5]

Il serait bien difficile de dégager les principes esthétiques du Théâtre d'art, animé par le trop jeune Paul Fort de 1890 à 1892, celui-ci se caractérisant par son éclectisme, sa volonté de redonner la parole aux poètes. Notons toutefois:

Innovation: l'obscurité dans la salle.
Décoration: *"La parole crée le décor comme le reste"* dit Paul Fort qui, avec ses amis peintres du groupe des Nabis (Vuillard, Paul Sérusier, Bonnard, Maurice Denis ...), affectionne les toiles peintes de style 'tapisserie'. Il mobilise parfois toute sa famille pour découper dans du papier doré, des blasons que l'on épinglera sur des rideaux de couleur unie.
Quant au répertoire symboliste, il est si maigre que le Théâtre d'Art doit monter le Victor Hugo du 'Théâtre en Liberté' ou les Parnassiens (Banville, Catulle Mendès) et multiplier les soirées poétiques avec, au programme, Shelley, Laforgue, Rimbaud, Jean Moréas...
On met en scène le biblique *Cantique des cantiques* dans une 'orchestration' verbale, musicale, colorée et... olfactive. Du parfum est vaporisé dans la salle, ce qui provoque fou rire et éternuements affectés...[6]

Quant à La Maison de l'Oeuvre (1893-1929), c'est à l'initiative personnelle de Lugné-Poe demandant à Maeterlinck de lui confier *Pelléas et Mélisande* pour une représentation unique (17 mai 1893) qu'elle doit sa naissance. Le ton poétique, les silences, l'inquiétude suggérée sont nouveaux au théâtre. S'il est vrai qu'on ne joue plus guère cette pièce, au profit de la composition de Debussy, il faut convenir qu'elle a lancé Lugné-Poe et que l'ensemble du théâtre de Maeterlinck relève d'une dramaturgie fort intéressante, avec sa théorie du "personnage sublime", celui qu'on ne voit pas mais dont on sent la présence obsédante.

Recommandant à ses comédiens la lenteur, l'immobilité, une sorte d'atonie, celui qu'on a surnommé "le clergyman somnambule" est moins un patron, un théoricien du théâtre, un dramaturge ou un metteur en scène génial qu'un animateur infatigable, toujours en quête d'oeuvres et d'idées nouvelles. Et son plus grand titre de gloire sera d'avoir, sinon découvert, du moins monté Maeterlinck, Claudel et surtout Jarry. A quel prix nous l'allons voir tout à l'heure.

Pourtant, cette successivité des esthétiques naturaliste et symboliste au théâtre ne laisse pas d'être trompeuse, en faussant la perspective historique. Il suffit de confronter les programmes du Théâtre Libre et de l'Oeuvre pour constater qu'aucun des deux ne s'est voué à une école en particulier, et qu'ils se sont partagé le mérite de monter les grands auteurs étrangers, qu'on serait bien en peine de qualifier. Il faudrait donc parler de simultanéité plutôt que de succession.

On pourrait se livrer à un petit jeu fort divertissant, sorte de *quid* ou de *trivial poursuit*. Qui a donné *La Nuit bergamasque*, trois actes en vers d'Emile Bergerat? *L'Evasion* de Villiers de l'Isle Adam? *Le Pain du péché*, quatre actes en vers de Paul Arène? *Le Cor fleuri* d'Ephraïm Mikael? *Le Baiser* de Banville? Antoine, en 1887-1888.

De même pour les étrangers. Qui a créé *La Puissance des ténèbres* de Tolstoï? *Les Revenants* et *Le Canard sauvage* d'Ibsen? *Les Tisserands* de Gerhart Hauptmann? *Le Pain d'autrui* de Tchékhov? *Mademoiselle Julie* de Strindberg?

Antoine, bien sûr. Mais à qui revient le mérite d'avoir monté *Un ennemi du peuple, Peer Gynt, Rosmersholm*, du même Ibsen? Et *Au delà des forces humaines* de Bjoernsterne Bjoernson? *Créanciers, Père* de Strindberg? Lugné-Poe, évidemment. De là des confusions auxquelles les historiens du théâtre ont bien du mal à échapper. C'est précisément le Théâtre Libre d'Antoine qui donnera aux symbolistes l'idée exacte du théâtre qu'ils rêvaient, mais qu'ils se refusaient de confier à la scène, si l'on en croit le jeune critique du *Mercure de France*, G.-A. Aurier. Rendant compte du *Canard sauvage* d'Ibsen, monté en 1891 par Antoine, il déclare que cette pièce inspirera "les jeunes dramaturges qui ont conscience de la nécessité d'une rénovation théâtrale. Il leur éclairera la voie de l'art synthétiste et idéaliste; il leur apprendra que l'observation réaliste n'a de valeur que comme auxiliaire de l'idée à exprimer. Et qu'aujourd'hui, ainsi que toujours, faire oeuvre d'art ce n'est pas pasticher la vie, mais créer des mythes viables."[7]

On ne saurait mieux souligner les lacunes du naturalisme et montrer le paradoxe fondamental sur lequel il se fonde au théâtre en dégageant de nouvelles perspectives. Si le naturalisme lasse, en effet, ce n'est pas tant par ses clichés abusifs, 'la tranche de vie', le morceau de boucherie et le foin sur la scène, c'est parce qu'il ne donne sur rien d'autre que le réel quotidien, se présentant comme un banal miroir, inutile réduplication de l'univers présent. De son côté, Mallarmé rêvait d'un 'spectacle futur', allusion à l'ensemble de l'univers, rejoignant le livre parfait, identifiant le livre et la scène. "*Théâtre*, en tant que *Mystère* par une opération appelée *Poésie*, cela à la faveur du *Livre*." Par là, il soulève une nouvelle ambiguïté du spectacle qui doit évoquer, suggérer, par des moyens propres à la représentation. Pourquoi, dès lors, ne pas lui préférer le livre, ce théâtre idéal qu'est le spectacle dans un fauteuil? Parce que seul le théâtre est susceptible de créer la communion du public dont rêve un véritable dramaturge. "Pièce-Office" notait Mallarmé dans les fragments manuscrits pour *Le Livre*.[8]

Depuis qu'il est entré en littérature, par la voie d'un concours littéraire de *L'Echo de Paris*, en 1893, où Ubu apparaît pour la première fois, sous le titre 'Guignol' (28 avril 1893), Jarry fréquente les 'mardis' de Rachilde au Mercure de France, et ceux de Mallarmé. Il suit, autant que faire se peut, la première saison de l'Oeuvre (dont, certainement, *Un ennemi du peuple* d'Ibsen, le 10 novembre), et rend compte de deux pièces montées par Lugné-Poe.

La première, *Ames solitaires*, drame en cinq actes de Gerhart Hauptmann, traduit par Alexandre Cohen, a d'abord été interdite par le ministre. Jarry se joint à Henri Baüer, Léon-Paul Fargue, Stuart Merrill, Paul Sérusier etc. pour protester contre l'arbitraire gouvernemental "qui n'est justifié ni par les tendances de la pièce, ni par les intentions injustement prêtées au public qui devait y assister, public littéraire et d'invités".[9] La mesure fut rapportée et la répétition générale put avoir lieu le 13 décembre au théâtre des Bouffes du Nord. Un rapport de police, que je reproduis pour la première fois, indique à ce propos:

(...) Environ 1000 personnes parmi lesquelles 200 femmes sont entrées. On a reconnu les anarchistes Rouanard, ancien directeur de *L'En dehors* et directeur de *L'Idée libre*, Jean Carrère, Alexandre Godichon dit Mercier (ce dernier se dit employé à la préfecture de la Seine).
(...) Après cet exposé, Georges Vanor a continué sa conférence et cherché à démontrer que la première représentation de cette oeuvre en Allemagne a été la fondation du théâtre terroriste.
Il a prouvé que Hauptmann n'avait pas été le porte parole de l'anarchisme dans son pays, mais au contraire celui du socialisme.
En terminant il a fait connaître que l'auteur était Gerhart Hauptmann et le traducteur Alexandre Cohen qui vient, a-t-il dit, d'être arrêté pour avoir chez lui un revolver chargé de 6 balles. Quel est donc celui parmi nous qui ne pourrait pas être arrêté pour un pareil fait.
La pièce a été ensuite interprétée très artistiquement et la fin de chaque tableau a été saluée par de nombreux applaudissements. Plusieurs fois les artistes ont été bissés.
La sortie s'est effectuée sans incidents: les spectateurs commentaient la pièce et beaucoup trouvaient qu'elle n'avait rien d'anarchiste mais qu'au contraire une bonne idée de morale et de religion s'en dégageait.[10]

Pour sa part, Jarry commente:

(...) Encore que j'aime plus au théâtre le déroulement du rêve en banderoles mauves ou fils de Vierge que la marche échiquière de thèses dont nulle n'est ni ne peut être neuve, chacune est trop asymptote à sa réalisation pour que Gerhart Hauptmann ne nous ait pas donné, au lieu de la tabletterie redoutée, une pièce de très haut Idéalisme, touchant plus même que *L'Ennemi du peuple*, parce que plus près de nous. Ceux qui vont les yeux baissés vers la terre dénombrent les lessives, tartines beurrées, pour eux réminiscences zoliques, inexpérients que l'Idéalisme s'exhausse plus aisément sur le marchepied du Réel qu'il ne se suspend à la Cardan en un nimbe; et que platoniciennement il fut défini d'un mode très large la Vie des Idées...[11]

Il n'est pas possible de suivre dans tous les détails son argumentation, particulièrement contorsionnée, visant à exalter l'idéalisme de la pièce, par opposition au réalisme d'Antoine. L'auteur l'a suffisamment marqué pour qu'il brosse de lui un portrait où, à nouveau, il le dresse face aux auteurs naturalistes:

(...) il pioche et déterre le vrai par-delà l'écorce de fer des contraires, au centre de Zola et d'Ibsen — quoique pourquoi restreindre à eux, moins modèles que pairs de vision innée, sa complexité? — l'amande joyau de l'Idéalisme et de l'Anarchie.[12]

La répétition générale de *Solness le constructeur*, d'Ibsen, eut lieu aux Bouffes du nord le 2 avril 1894. Le policier de service informe le Préfet que 400 personnes y ont assisté.

> Ce public était en grande partie composé d'artistes, de journalistes et d'hommes de lettres. M. Camille Mauclair a fait avant la représentation une conférence sur la pièce d'Ibsen. (...) Solness était un architecte non pour satisfaire les riches qui le faisaient travailler mais bien pour propager l'art de même que l'acteur joue non pour la satisfaction de quelques riches flâneurs qui viennent digérer sur un fauteuil respectable mais bien plutôt pour propager les leçons de morale qui se dégagent des pièces de théâtre. Applaudissements.
> En résumé [dit-il], c'est une pièce empreinte tout au long de ce socialisme mystique que l'on trouve dans *L'Ennemi du peuple* mais d'un socialisme plus voilé et laissant moins percer cette haine du riche que l'on trouve dans *L'Ennemi du peuple*...[13]

Dans son compte-rendu, Jarry approuve la conférence de Mauclair, loue le jeu de Lugné-Poe qui "incarne l'âme de faiblesse et de force tressées de Maître Solness" et le félicite pour l'intelligence de sa mise en scène, qui fait l'ellipse du mannequin de Solness précipité par la foule.[14]
S'il n'a pu rendre compte de tous les spectacles donnés par l'Oeuvre, nous savons que Jarry les a suivis avec attention. Le 30 octobre 1894, il entre en contact avec son directeur, pour lui demander des places en échange du service de *L'Ymagier*, la revue d'art qu'il dirige avec Rémy de Gourmont. Deux ans après, il est devenu suffisamment familier avec lui pour lui proposer de monter *Ubu roi*, oeuvre pour laquelle il trace la mise en scène, les décors et les costumes. Devenu le secrétaire-factotum de Lugné, il n'aura de cesse de faire jouer sa pièce, tout en contribuant aux activités de l'Oeuvre, en particulier lors de la représentation de *Peer Gynt*, pièce d'Ibsen dans laquelle il figure un des trolls. Depuis trois ans, il a pu affiner sa conception de la mise en scène, ce pourquoi il propose de monter *Peer Gynt* "d'une façon simple et même sordide."[15] De fait, il s'est, peu à peu, constitué un corps de doctrine.
En 1891, il a pu lire l'article de Pierre Quillard, "De l'inutilité absolue de la mise en scène exacte", où celui-ci démontrait l'inanité du naturalisme au théâtre, déclarant:

> *La parole crée le décor comme le reste* (...) *Le décor doit être une simple fiction ornementale qui complète l'illusion par des analogies de couleurs et de lignes avec le drame.* Le plus souvent, il suffira d'un fond et de quelques draperies mobiles pour donner l'impression de l'infinie multiplicité du temps et du lieu. Le spectateur (...) s'abandonnera tout entier à la volonté du poète et y verra, selon son âme, des figures terribles et charmantes et des pays de mensonge où nul autre que lui ne pénétrera: le théâtre sera ce qu'il doit être: *un prétexte au rêve*.[16]

Jarry n'aura pas une grande distance à parcourir pour dénoncer, en septembre 1896, l'inutilité absolue du théâtre au théâtre! Ce qui, en bonne logique, devait le conduire à préférer la vie à la représentation (ce dont témoignera sa chronique 'Gestes' à la *Revue blanche* en 1901). En vérité, ses conceptions dramatiques, où les paradoxes abondent, se sont affirmées à propos de la geste d'*Ubu*, composée et représentée en marionnettes et en ombres, au lycée de Rennes en 1888 (*Ubu intime*), remise en forme avec les frères Morin en 1894, parachevée pour la représentation d'*Ubu roi* à l'Oeuvre. Elles aboutissent à une esthétique de l'abstrait, préfigurant notre théâtre contemporain.

Tout d'abord, le théâtre n'a que faire des consignes et des principes établis. Il doit s'affirmer comme théâtre et ne pas donner l'illusion du réel.

Il n'existe que par le public à qui il donne "le plaisir actif de créer aussi un peu à mesure et de prévoir".[17] C'est dire que, comme Pierre Quillard, il exclut la reproduction du réel, 'la pièce bien faite', dont on connaît les péripéties à l'avance, et le théâtre de Boulevard, fait pour digérer.

Seul peut écrire pour la scène celui qui a eu la vision d'un personnage n'ayant aucun précédent ni dans les livres, ni dans la vie. Ainsi, dira-t-il (en reprenant un argument de Quillard), Hamlet "est plus vivant qu'un homme qui passe, car il est plus compliqué avec plus de synthèse, et même seul vivant, car il est une abstraction qui marche" (p. 412).

Ce personnage doit être unique, synthèse complexe de différents caractères, supérieur en cela à l'individu vivant, suscitant les comparses et le décor autour de sa personne. "Que chaque héros traîne après soi son décor (...) cela prouve sans plus que l'auteur a retourné ses créatures et mis leur âme en dehors; l'âme est un tic." (II: 416)

S'il n'est pas naturel (c'est-à-dire si la pièce ne se déroule pas en plein air), le décor ne doit pas chercher à reproduire la nature mais, au contraire, tendre à l'éternel et à l'intemporel, pour laisser libre jeu à l'imagination du spectateur. De la même façon, les objets, qui sont partie intégrante du décor, seront aussi artificiels que possible. Après avoir envisagé un décor héraldique pour *César Antéchrist* (sur quoi je reviendrai), Jarry vante les mérites, autrement plus faciles à obtenir, du décor naïf, par "celui qui ne sait pas peindre", et finalement lance le concept de "décor abstrait", ce qui ne signifie pas absence de décor mais synthèse de tous les possibles.

Aussitôt, avec une belle abnégation quant à sa fonction de metteur en scène, Lugné-Poe reprend la proposition au bond:

> Pas de décor ou peu, prismique ou autre, et que le mot de mise en scène soit rayé à jamais de la liste des personnages! Le plus fort des metteurs en scène ne peut pas être un artiste, puisque sa besogne est celle d'un ajusteur panoramique, qui recréera au mieux sa compréhension de Munckazy ou de Meissonier pour une vision commune, uniforme cependant, c'est-à-dire pour une théorie de regards différemment placés et artistes.[18]

De fait, Jarry pense explicitement au choix opéré avec ses amis Sérusier, Ranson, Vuillard, Bonnard, Toulouse-Lautrec, qui ont tous mis la main à l'unique toile de scène d'*Ubu roi*, malheureusement introuvable aujourd'hui, mais dont nous connaissons la fonction et la description par Jarry lui-même dans son discours préliminaire à la première représentation:

> Nous aurons d'ailleurs un décor parfaitement exact, car de même qu'il est un procédé facile pour situer une pièce dans l'Eternité, à savoir de faire par exemple tirer en l'an mille et tant des coups de revolver, vous verrez des portes s'ouvrir sur des plaines de neige sous un ciel bleu, des cheminées garnies de pendules se fendre afin de servir de portes, et des palmiers verdir au pied des lits, pour que les broutent de petits éléphants perchés sur des étagères. (p. 400)

L'acteur doit se faire le plus impersonnel possible, de manière à ne pas imposer sa présence, sa propre interprétation. Aussi Jarry conseille-t-il l'usage du masque, et de prendre la voix du rôle. Là encore, Lugné-Poe, ravi de l'aubaine puisqu'elle va dans le sens de son propre jeu, reprend l'idée à son compte: "Pour le comédien, la leçon est plus simple, plus difficile aussi. Il doit oublier qu'il est comédien, se souvenir des premières fois où, enfant, il assistait au théâtre en pieux spectateur, et, rejetant en bloc toutes les mauvaises éducations, devenir brusquement UN — *un quelconque! bras ballants, geste immobile.*" (*ibidem*)

Mais il ne faudrait pas déduire de tels principes que Jarry, s'adressant à une élite de spectateurs, ne tienne pas compte des progrès de la réalisation scénique contemporaine. Au contraire, il prend note des effets de la lumière électrique, récemment introduite au théâtre, pour en déduire qu'elle peut, à elle seule, servir de décor, ou, en tout cas, produire des effets divers sur les masques, donnant relief au personnage, créant des ombres gigantales, aplanissant des surfaces.

Dans sa correspondance avec Lugné-Poe, Jarry tente de lui faire accepter toutes les innovations possibles (parfois dans un but intéressé) pour concrétiser cette troisième voie synthétique, qui dépasse l'opposition du naturalisme et du symbolisme, pour tendre vers le théâtre de l'avenir.

Après avoir examiné les théories dramaturgiques de Jarry, il est bon de jeter un oeil sur ses réalisations concrètes.

Sa première pièce, publiée par le *Mercure de France* en juillet 1894, *Haldernablou*, semble relever, par la forme et le ton, du symbolisme le plus exalté, particulièrement dans les paroles du choeur. Pièce germinative, d'une importance capitale, quoique peu estimée et jamais représentée (à ma connaissance), puisqu'on y trouve, à l'état embryonnaire, tous les éléments que Jarry développera dans son oeuvre future. Mais, déjà, la thématique symboliste de l'adelphisme épuré par l'ascèse, c'est-à-dire, en termes vulgaires, d'une homosexualité passive; le décor, l'atmosphère noble et tragiques; sont pervertis par des éléments trivialement modernes, comme le décor de la gare

Saint-Lazare, le tramway, ou la dame des W.C. Mélange du bas et du sublime, caractéristique du grotesque, accentué par l'écho, extraordinaire à cette date, des images de Lautréamont, telles: "l'araignée des préjugés", "le hibou aux paupières de soie" etc.

Dès sa première publication, l'humour de Jarry pointe l'oreille. Il pervertit le symbolisme, et l'on sent bien qu'il ne s'en tiendra pas là. C'est, effectivement, ce qui se produit avec son second drame, *César Antéchrist*, publié, par fragments, en revue, en 1894, et repris en volume l'année suivante, puisqu'il contient, en guise d'acte central, une version très abrégée d'*Ubu roi*. C'est dire, d'emblée, que la thématique la plus exagérément symboliste, ayant trait à la figure de l'Apocalypse, se trouve incarnée par le personnage, ô combien trivial, du Père Ubu!

C'est à l'acte II, dit "acte héraldique" ou encore intitulé "orle", terme du blason désignant la bordure étroite de l'écu, que Jarry imagine un décor entièrement emprunté au langage codé des armoiries. On a conservé trois dessins de Jarry lui-même, permettant d'imaginer ce qu'était, pour lui, ce décor en blason.[19] Chaque scène se déroule sur une toile de fond aux couleurs d'un blason. Ainsi la première est "de sable à un Roi d'or", c'est-à-dire qu'un personnage royal vêtu de couleurs dorées se détache sur une toile de fond noire. A la scène suivante, c'est une licorne d'argent, représentée dans l'attitude de la marche, qui paraît. Pour la scène quatre, la toile de fond change. Elle est désormais de vair, garnie de fourrures en forme de clochetons, disposées tête-bêche sur des lignes horizontales. Les figurants et les personnage sont eux-mêmes des écus, disposés de différentes manières sur la scène. On imagine la lourdeur d'un tel dispositif scénique, qui, de plus, demande une connaissance minimale de la langue du blason pour être compris convenablement. Une telle tentative pour renouveler le décor de théâtre dans un sens symboliste ne manque pas d'intérêt. "Nous avons essayé des décors *héraldiques*, c'est-à-dire désignant d'une teinte unie et uniforme toute une scène ou un acte, les personnages passant harmoniques sur ce champ de blason" déclare Jarry dans son article 'De l'inutilité du théâtre au théâtre' (407). Outre que ces imaginations n'ont jamais été transposées à la scène, à distance, Jarry juge ce dispositif puéril, parce qu'il limite le nombre de formes et de couleurs, alors qu'une simple toile grise, neutre pour le metteur en scène, autorise toutes les projections du spectateur, en fonction du texte dramatique.

De fait, seule la présentation d'*Ubu roi* par le Théâtre de l'Oeuvre traduit concrètement les idées de Jarry sur le théâtre. Les représentations antérieures, en marionnettes, si elles ont pu influencer la mise en scène de Lugné-Poe, n'entrent pas dans notre propos, puisque l'auteur se pliait, alors, aux codes du castelet.

Observons, tout d'abord, que cette première n'allait pas de soi, et qu'elle n'était pas conçue comme une révolution dramatique mais plutôt comme une plaisanterie bruyante. Malgré tous les efforts déployés par Jarry, Lugné-Poe renâclait. Pour lui, la pièce était inclassable, et il craignait un échec préjudiciable à sa jeune entreprise. En témoigne la lettre que Rachilde lui adressa le 15 novembre 1896:

> Voyons! Si vous ne sentiez pas un *succès* quand vous avez accepté cette pièce, pourquoi, vous, directeur de théâtre, sachant de quoi se forme le succès, qui est, quelquefois, simplement un grand *tapage*, l'avez-vous prise?
> Moi, je ne suis jamais bien au courant de ce qui se passe parce que je vis très peu et pas, surtout, dans vos sacrés milieux journalistiques mais, cependant, j'entends dire et redire chez moi que toute la jeune génération, y compris quelques bons vieux aimant la blague, est dans l'attente de cette représentation (...)[20]

Elle poursuit en conseillant de pousser la mise en scène vers le guignol, en faisant relier les acteurs aux frises du théâtre par des guindes. Ce que Jarry parviendra à éviter, comme il l'indique dans sa conférence préliminaire, car il s'agissait, pour lui, de transposer l'oeuvre des lycéens en un théâtre pour adultes, non l'inverse. Selon Rachilde, il n'était question que d'une belle occasion de rire, peu importait la manière.

A la réflexion, plusieurs années après, de tout le répertoire nouveau monté par Lugné-Poe, c'est finalement *Ubu roi* qui ressortira comme l'oeuvre la plus marquante. Tel est le sentiment d'un Henri Ghéon, qu'on ne peut soupçonner de partialité, lors d'une conférence au public du Vieux-Colombier, en 1923:

> Savez-vous quel est, à mon sens, le titre principal de l'Oeuvre à la reconnaissance des amis de l'art dramatique? La représentation d'*Ubu roi*. (...) Qu'on lui attribue le sens qu'on voudra, *Ubu roi* de Jarry, c'est du théâtre pur, synthétique, poussant jusqu'au scandale l'usage avoué de la convention, créant, en marge du réel, une réalité avec des *signes*.[21]

En somme, poussant à leur comble les voies réaliste et symboliste, les mêlant en une salade étourdissante, Jarry a retrouvé les principes du théâtre, son autonomie irréductible.

Au moment où s'affrontaient les pièces bien faites, à thèse ou à idées, il présente la geste épique inventée par des enfants, d'une telle indigence qu'elle subsume tout le théâtre épique. La grande force d'*Ubu roi* réside dans la pureté absolue d'un schéma dramatique réduit à la conquête du pouvoir, au règne terrifique, et à la fuite de l'usurpateur poursuivi par l'héritier légitime, dont rien ne vient entraver le déroulement. Aucune référence historique, aucune motivation psychologique, aucune explication politique ou idéologique. *Ubu roi* est, littéralement, irrécupérable.

Contrairement à la tradition, la parodie n'a aucune fonction critique. Elle se sert de scènes dont l'effet est assuré, inspirées du théâtre classique ou populaire, du vaudeville ou de guignol, pour le seul plaisir du spectateur.

Et d'insister sur ce qui a toujours été proscrit au théâtre, la matérialité de la vie: déjeuner, orgie, cauchemar d'indigestion etc.

Inversement, Jarry montre les vertus du théâtre pris pour lui-même, comme une succession de gestes et d'actions, de signes appartenant au seul univers dramatique: scène de la trappe, combats, revue des troupes, course au trésor etc.

Si les acteurs ont le jeu épuré et stylisé de la marionnette, incarnant les archétypes du théâtre shakespearien, ils construisent un personnage qui se dissout aussitôt, réduit à une simple silhouette. Quant à Ubu, le personnage unique, autour duquel gravitent les comparses, il est le contraire même d'un héros, par sa totale négativité, pour ne pas dire nullité. En fait, guidé par ses seuls instincts, il se réduit aux fonctions primitives, manger, boire et dormir. Par quoi il donne prise au mythe, étant l'autre honni, l'hétérogène que chacun nourrit en soi et repousse par bienséance.

Enfin le langage illustre la synthèse et le dépassement des tendances mimétiques et idéalistes alors aux prises. On se souvient d'une des scènes les plus provocantes. Gémier (l'interprète d'Ubu), voulant entrer dans la forteresse de Thorn, mettait une clé imaginaire dans le main d'un garde, fi-gurant la porte. Il la faisait tourner, cric, crac, le figurant pivotait, Ubu entrait dans la prison. Ainsi le jeu naturel des enfants venait résoudre les antinomies de la mise en scène. Il n'en va pas autrement sur le plan verbal, avec le langage d'Ubu, dont je ne donnerai qu'un exemple, le fameux mot, répété trente-trois fois. Il n'est pas réaliste, puisqu'il est doté d'une épenthèse en R. Mais il n'est pas davantage symbolique, puisqu'il est chargé, si je puis dire, du poids de la matière fécale. C'est donc bien l'alliance des contraires, et quelque chose de plus, que manifeste cette invention verbale.

Il n'est donc pas exagéré de dire qu'en portant à la scène, sans y rien changer, la création de quelques adolescents, Jarry a indiqué la voie qui rénovera la dramaturgie française pour de longues années.

Notes

1. Voir Aderer, *Le Théâtre à côté*, préface de F. Sarcey, Librairies imprimeries réunies, 1894.

2. Voir Augustin Filon, *De Dumas à Rostand. Esquisse du mouvement dramatique contemporain*. A. Colin, 1898.

3. Voir Dorothy Knowles, *La réaction idéaliste au théâtre depuis 1890*, Genève: Droz, 1934.

4. Voir Albert Thibaudet, *Histoire de la littérature française de 1789 à nos jours* (Stock, 1936), quatrième partie, 'La génération de 1885, le théâtre', pp. 493-514; Henri Clouard, *Histoire de la littérature française du symbolisme à nos jours*, t. I: 'De 1885 à 1914', nouvelle éd. corrigée, 1947, pp. 126-136, 271-290; *Histoire des spectacles*, sous la direction de Guy Dumur (Gallimard, Encyclopédie de la Pléiade, 1965), pp. 1079-1102 par Georges Lerminier; Jacqueline de Jomaron, *Le Théâtre en France*, t. II (Armand Colin, 1989), pp. 192-214: 'Reconstruire le réel et suggérer l'indicible' par Jean-Pierre Sarrazac; André Degaine, *Histoire du théâtre dessinée* (Nizet, 1972).

5. André Degaine, *op. cit.* pp. 290-291.

6. *Ibidem*, pp. 306-307.

7. Dans *Mercure de France*, 1891.

8. Jacques Schérer: *Le 'Livre' de Mallarmé*, premières recherches sur des documents inédits, préface d'Henri Mondor (Gallimard, 1957).

9. Protestation publiée par *Le Journal* du 14 décembre 1893, reproduite dans: Alfred Jarry, *Oeuvres complètes*, Bibliothèque de la Pléiade (1987), t. II, p. 577.

10. Archives du Musée de la police, 1, bis rue des Carmes à Paris, dossier Lugné-Poe, Da 168.

11. Alfred Jarry, 'Ames solitaires', *L'Art littéraire*, n. s. n° 1 et 2, janvier-février 1894, pp. 21-25. Reproduit dans les *Oeuvres complètes*, Pléiade, t. I (1972), p. 1003.

12. Alfred Jarry: 'Gerhart Hauptmann', *Portraits du prochain siècle* (Edmond Girard, 1894), pp. 88-89, repris dans les *O.C.*, Pléiade, t. II, pp. 577-578.

13. Archives du Musée de la police, dossier Lugné-Poe, Da 168.

14. Alfred Jarry: 'Théâtre de l'Oeuvre. — *Solness le constructeur*', *L'Art littéraire*, n. s. n° 5-6 (mai-juin 1894), pp. 93-94, repris dans *O.C.* Pléiade, t. I, pp. 1008-1009.

15. Alfred Jarry, lettre à Lugné-Poe d'août 1896, *O.C.* t. I p. 1052.

16. Pierre Quillard: 'De l'inutilité absolue de la mise en scène exacte', dans: *Revue d'art dramatique*, 1er mai 1891.

17. Alfred Jarry: 'De l'inutilité du théâtre au théâtre', dans: *Mercure de France*, septembre 1896, repris dans *O.C.* Pléiade, t. I, p. 406. Pour tout ce qui concerne ces questions de dramaturgie, nous citons d'après cette édition, en indiquant la pagination entre parenthèses dans le corps de l'article.

18. A. Lugné-Poe: 'A propos de l'inutilité du théâtre au théâtre', dans: *Mercure de France*, octobre 1896, pp. 96-97.

19. Voir Michel Arrivé, *Peintures, gravures et dessins d'Alfred Jarry* (Paris, Collège de Pataphysique et Cercle français du livre, 1968), et notre commentaire dans: Henri Behar: *Jarry dramaturge* (Paris: Nizet, 1980), pp. 33-34.

20. Lettre de Rachilde à Lugné-Poe, publiée en fac-similé par Henri Bordillon dans *L'Etoile-absinthe*, 4e tournée, décembre 1979. Lugné-Poe la cite, partiellement, dans *Acrobaties* (Gallimard, 1932).

21. Henri Ghéon, *Dramaturgie d'hier et de demain* (Lyon: Vitte, 1963), pp. 109-110. Cité par Henri Behar, *op. cit.* p. 74.

Frank Salaün
SPECTRES ET INCARNATIONS DU BOURGEOIS:
QUELQUES REMARQUES SUR LA SIGNIFICATION
DU THÉÂTRE EN FRANCE AUTOUR DE 1894

Alfred Jarry

En 1894, Alfred Jarry a 21 ans. Il n'a connu ni la guerre de 1870 ni la Commune. Les espoirs placés dans le peuple et dans un art social — on pense à Courbet — lui sont à peu près étrangers. Il appartient à une génération d'artistes qui a tendance à douter de la politique et des mouvements sociaux, et revendique l'autonomie de l'art. Le repoussoir c'est le "bourgeois", la tentation c'est l'anarchisme.

Les lettres de Jarry à Lugné-Poe, le créateur du Théâtre de l'Oeuvre, révèlent son enthousiasme et ses stratégies. En 1896, Jarry évoque la mise en scène de *Peer Gynt*, d'Ibsen et de *Ubu roi* qui sera joué le 10 décembre. En août il écrit:

> Je pense que vous ne vous découragez pas et que nous allons monter *Peer Gynt*. Il est de ce drame comme de ceux de Shakespeare, qui gagnent à être montés d'une façon simple et même sordide et autrement ressembleraient au *Tour du monde en 80 jours* et autres pièces du Châtelet.[1]

L'exemple a son importance. Cette adaptation de Jules Verne a en effet été représentée 1550 fois entre 1874, l'année de la première, et 1898.[2] Le public raffole des spectacles où les progrès techniques lui apparaissent sur scène, suscitant surprises et frayeurs. Avec *Le Tour du monde en 80 jours* il contemple le progrès — les trains, les bateaux... — et ressent l'accélération du temps et la maîtrise de l'espace. Cela conforte en même temps son européocentrisme et sa bonne conscience colonialiste. Jarry manifeste donc ici un double refus; refus du théâtre grand spectacle, mais aussi du vaudeville et de ses décors fouillés. Il est vrai que dans les deux cas les éléments matériels ont tendance à l'emporter. Il s'oppose en fait à une définition large du théâtre qui englobe à la fois les textes dramatiques, les opérettes, voire les revues. La hiérarchie se fait de plus en plus en fonction d'une nouvelle forme de célébrité, favorisée par la presse et la centralisation des spectacles. Un auteur, un acteur ou même un chanteur, peut faire fortune s'il est à la mode. Cela nourrit d'ailleurs certains reproches adressés à Bruant qui tout en se distinguant du spectacle bourgeois s'enrichit.

La position de Jarry, qui rejoint en partie le mot d'ordre d'élévation, de respiritualisation des symbolistes[3], implique aussi le refus d'un certain goût et d'un type de public. En septembre son énergie n'a pas faibli: "Enfin vous allez revenir et on répétera *Peer Gynt*. Ce sera le meilleur démenti à ceux qui disent que ce n'est pas montable...".[4] Dans le même temps le projet *UBU* se précise. Le 1er août il s'agit du rôle de Bougrelas:

... cette idée d'un gosse dans le rôle de Bougrelas... Ce serait peut-être
un clou pour *UBU*, exciterait des vieilles dames et ferait crier au
scandale certains; en tout cas, ça ferait faire attention à des gens; et
puis ça ne s'est jamais vu et je crois qu'il faut que l' "Oeuvre"
monopolise toutes les innovations.[5]

Les stratégies que l'on repère ici, indiquent en outre, que le public correspon-
dant à l'art indépendant n'existe pas encore, et qu'une nouvelle conception
du rôle de l'auteur, du texte et de la mise en scène se dessine. Pour les
"théâtres à-côté" la création passe par une rupture avec les goûts dominants.
Il s'agit non seulement d'inventer un nouveau théâtre — et la promotion de
l'expérimentation définit partiellement l'avant-gardisme — mais aussi un
nouveau public.
L'apparition à la fin du siècle de la mise en scène au sens fort, coïncide avec
le renforcement de la "position" d'artiste, et l'affirmation d'une ambition
illimitée en art, dont la formule "l'art pour l'art" n'est qu'une approximation.[6]
Le recours à des textes d'auteurs étrangers, y compris allemands, en pleine
période d'exaltation patriotique, s'explique en partie de cette façon. L'artiste
tel qu'il se voit, appartient d'abord au monde de la création. Pour le théâtre
"d'art" — par opposition à un théâtre à la fois conformiste et commercial — ce
qui est réputé impossible à monter est par définition intéressant comme
forme de dépassement. Expérimentation et distinction se complètent ici. Il
s'agit de faire autre chose, avec toute l'ambiguïté que cela comporte: inventer
et se passer de ce qui existe, nier ou dépasser les formes convenues. La suite
de la lettre du 1er août va bien dans ce sens:

Vallette agite dans le Mercure qui va paraître des idées de théâtre en
plein air, une ou deux fois par an, dans un bois? (...) Il y aurait peut-
être des choses étonnantes pour l' "Oeuvre" et un public cycliste qu'on
ferait payer jusqu'à la mort.

Création et opportunisme semblent être amenés à se compléter. Les formules
nouvelles sont bonnes à prendre. La mode est aux balades à bicyclette — Jarry
partage l'engouement pour ce nouveau mode de transport — eh bien
pourquoi pas un théâtre dans les bois?
La conception de la place de l'art a évolué dans la seconde partie du XIXe
siècle, surtout après 1870. Jarry ici, ne se positionne ni comme Baudelaire, ni
comme Courbet, ni même comme Gauguin avec lequel il a certains points
communs. Chez lui, la subversion est à la fois réaction et création. Dans *Ubu
roi*, on retrouve — singulièrement déformés — certains thèmes dominants ou
censurés, du théâtre de l'époque. La pièce est centrée sur un couple,
monsieur et madame Ubu, appelés suivant le langage populaire, Père Ubu
et Mère Ubu. L'homme est peureux, bête, grossier, obsédé par la possession,
sur un mode en fait alimentaire. La femme est calculatrice, ambitieuse,
décidée. Comme dans certains vaudevilles, elle pousse son époux à
l'ascension sociale. "Comment, Père Ubu, vous êtes content de votre sort?",

demande-t-elle, insidieuse, avant de suggérer: "Qui t'empêche de massacrer toute la famille et de te mettre à leur place?" Et, alors que Ubu rétorque qu'il a "un cul comme les autres": "A ta place, ce cul, je voudrais l'installer sur un trône. Tu pourrais augmenter indéfiniment tes richesses, manger fort souvent de l'andouille et rouler carrosse par les rues." (Acte I, scène 1)
Le couple, la dépendance d'Ubu par rapport à sa femme — "si je passais par la casserole, qui te raccommoderait tes fonds de culotte?" — l'ascension sociale, l'argent et l'univers guerrier sont associés à la merde et aux fonctions organiques, ce qui rappelle très fortement la culture anarchiste, à commencer par le vocabulaire qui s'apparente à l'argot dont l'usage était prôné par les anarchistes, comme le montrent les articles de Pouget dans Le Père Peinard, et dont Bruant fera le dictionnaire. "La chanson du décervelage", qui n'est pas reprise dans l'édition originale, prend à contre-pied la mode des chansons dans les spectacles — opérettes, vaudevilles — et se rapproche du ton populaire et anti-bourgeois. "Voyez, voyez la machin' tourner/ Voyez, voyez la cervelle sauter/ Voyez, voyez les Rentiers trembler..."[7] "La Ravachole", cette chanson en l'honneur du célèbre anarchiste que publie en 1894 l'Almanach du Père Peinard, résume bien cette tradition par son refrain, sur l'air de "La Carmagnole" et de "ça ira", qui dit en substance: "Dansons la Ravachole/ Vive le son d'l'explosion!/Ah, ça ira.../Tous les bourgeois goûtr'ont d'la bombe/ Ah, ça ira.../Tous les bourgeois on les saut'ra!"
Mais la représentation du peuple a aussi évolué depuis Hugo et Michelet. Comme les théoriciens anarchistes, Jarry semble ne croire ni aux lois qui sont un piège, ni aux ressources des masses abruties par l'idéologie dominante et les progrès matériels.[8] Ses réponses aux questions de l'enquête sur "L'Alsace-Lorraine et l'état actuel des esprits", publiées en 1897 dans le Mercure de France — alors que le discours revanchard est toujours aussi fort — sont caractéristiques.[9]

1. C'est la première fois [dit-il], que je lis le mot "traité de Francfort".
2. Le peuple parle toujours autant de l'Alsace-Lorraine, mais il n'en pense probablement rien.
3. Étant né en 1873, la guerre de 1870 est dans mon souvenir trois ans au-dessous de l'oubli absolu. Il me paraît vraisemblable que cet événement n'a jamais eu lieu, simple invention pédagogique en vue de favoriser les bataillons scolaires.
4. Je demande la guerre, la guerre immédiate (je ne suis point soldat). Mais 1. pour des raisons nombreuses elle n'aura pas lieu; 2. si elle imminait, ceux-là seuls désirant la restitution de l'Alsace et de la Lorraine qui, propriétaires là-bas, ne peuvent rentrer en France qu'après vente (à perte craignent-ils) de leurs terres, un terme simple à leurs réclamations serait, sinon leur massacre général, au moins la confiscation de leurs biens.
Quant à l'opinion de la jeunesse et du pays, je crois que cette question ne les intéresse pas, moi non plus d'ailleurs, ni la question ni celle de savoir ce qu'ils en pensent.[10]

On reconnaît ici des thèmes anarchistes, mais Jarry, comme beaucoup d'artistes à la fin du siècle, n'en conserve qu'une part, celle qui conforte son appartenance au monde authentique de l'art. D'ailleurs les anarchistes qui passent à l'acte — la grande vague d'attentats terroristes correspond aux années 1892-1894 — lui paraissent à la fois naïfs et incultes, comme s'ils se trompaient sur la nature du langage anarchiste en le prenant à la lettre.[11] Le rejet de l'armée, de l'argent, de la nation sont, dans la perspective de la "vie d'artiste" à la fin du siècle, rejetés comme les instruments d'un discours idéologique. Dans *Ubu roi*[12], on constate que l'obsession de l'argent, l'enthousiasme pour la guerre chez les soldats, les valeurs militaires, et les différents élans collectifs — indiqués en particulier par les "Vive la Mère Ubu!"(p. 356); "Vive le Père Ubu!" (p. 361) "Vive Dieu!" (p. 364) "Vive le roi!" (p. 367), "Vive la guerre!"(p. 377), "Vive la Pologne!" (p. 377).... qui ponctuent la pièce — sont renvoyés à la bêtise et à la merde. Comme si partant des *Lettres persanes* on avait dissout tout moyen de synthèse dans la fable des Troglodytes, si ce n'est le constat pessimiste et moqueur d'un cercle vicieux.[13]

Jarry n'est donc pas vraiment représentatif du théâtre en France en 1894[14], il est sur une voie nouvelle liée à la métamorphose de l'idéal de la vie d'artiste, mais il en révèle, par la subversion qu'il pratique, par l'écart qu'il impose, les forces constitutives.

Les ambiguïtés du vaudeville: Feydeau

Il est vrai qu'au XIXe siècle le théâtre joue un très grand rôle dans la société française. On va voir des pièces, les journaux, les conversations, les chansons s'en font l'écho, et inversement le théâtre parle de cette société moderne; il y a complémentarité. De cette façon la société ne fait pas que se conforter, elle s'interroge sur elle-même.

La figure du "bourgeois" — la problématique des classes moyennes en mouvement — tient une place centrale dans le théâtre autour de 1894. Elle sous-tend le rapport entre le public et les pièces. Le cas du vaudeville est de ce point de vue particulièrement instructif. En 1894 c'est toujours l'un des genres florissants. On estime à dix mille le nombre de vaudevilles joués au XIXe siècle.[15]

Feydeau après des débuts difficiles, entre 1881 et 1892 — à part *Tailleur pour dame* (1887) — remporte à partir de 1892 une série de succès. Entre février et décembre 1894 quatre de ses pièces sont montées. Avec lui, sur les traces de Labiche, le vaudeville s'affine et s'affirme, grâce à des procédés et des thèmes qui touchent très efficacement un public nombreux.[16]

De quoi parlent ses pièces? Pourquoi le public y réagit-il si favorablement? Elles parlent de l'univers bourgeois, pas seulement du bourgeois-type caractérisé par un niveau de vie, mais aussi de l'attraction et de la répulsion qui sont liées à son mode de vie. Le vaudeville repose — et cela de façon sans doute plus forte dans le dernier quart du siècle — sur les ambiguïtés du modèle bourgeois. Il n'est ni tout à fait de plain-pied, ni véritablement en porte-à-faux avec lui. Il tient compte de la censure et des pressions diverses du pouvoir, de l'exigence de rentabilité des directeurs de théâtres, et du goût du public. Le public choisit son théâtre par l'accueil qu'il réserve aux pièces, situation que le théâtre "à côté" cherche à renverser. Le vaudeville est par conséquent davantage révélateur d'un certain état de l'opinion que de l'auteur en tant qu'individu. En effet, le rire a une histoire. On ne rit pas des mêmes choses, ou du moins pas pour les mêmes raisons, jamais tout à fait de la même façon.

Dans *Un fil à la patte* — monté en novembre 1894 — Feydeau enchaîne les quiproquos à partir du moment où Bois-d'Enghien venu pour annoncer son mariage et rompre avec sa maîtresse, n'en a pas le courage.[17] Celle-ci ne manquera pas l'occasion, au moment de la signature du contrat, de faire scandale, en s'arrangeant pour que Bois-D'Enghien soit surpris avec elle par tous les invités.

L'envie de s'encanailler traverse d'ailleurs de nombreuses pièces. Dans *Un fil à la patte*, de nouveau, Lucette, la maîtresse de Bois-d'Enghien est chanteuse de Café-concert. Elle représente la tentation du bourgeois. Au début de la pièce, une amie lui annonce qu'elle va se marier, devenir duchesse de la Courtille et qu'à partir de maintenant elle aura le sentiment de s'encanailler en venant la voir. Lucette vexée s'exclame: "Ah! bah! ça fera peut-être une petite dame de moins, ça ne fera pas une grande dame de plus." (Acte I, scène VII) Et à la fin de la pièce, par un retournement remarquable, Viviane la fiancée de Bois-d'Enghien qui jusqu'à lors n'était pas attirée par lui, le trouve désormais beaucoup plus attirant et décide contre l'avis de sa mère de l'épouser (Acte III, scène VIII). Conformément à l'acte II, où elle disait déjà: "...c'est ça l'amour! C'est quand on peut dire: 'Ah! ah cet homme-là, vous auriez bien voulu l'avoir... Eh bien, c'est moi qui l'ai, et vous ne l'aurez pas!'" (Acte II, scène III); elle déclare: "Qu'importe ce qui s'est passé. Je n'ai vu qu'une chose: c'est que vous étiez bien tel que j'avais rêvé mon mari!" (Acte III, scène VIII)

Par la construction multipliée de quiproquos, le comique de situation l'emporte, le comique de mots et le talent des acteurs le complètent. C'est cet aspect du vaudeville qui retiendra l'attention de Bergson qui en propose, en 1899, une interprétation structurelle de type vitaliste. Pour lui, le quiproquo suppose une "interférence de séries" qui aboutit à "une mécanisation de la vie". Le vaudeville conclut Bergson,

> est à la vie réelle ce que le pantin articulé est à l'homme qui marche, une exagération très artificielle d'une certaine raideur naturelle des choses. Ce n'est guère qu'un jeu, subordonné, comme tous les jeux, à une convention d'abord acceptée.[18]

Or, s'il est vrai que le vaudeville fonctionne comme un système, celui-ci n'est efficace que s'il a un rapport avec un tissu social plausible. La situation des personnages correspond à la fois à un moment donné du déroulement de l'histoire, et à un rapport de forces à l'intérieur d'un système social. Le public assiste bien sûr à un enchaînement de scènes, mais il décode en même temps un ensemble de signes, matériels ou verbaux qui appartiennent à l'univers élargi des classes moyennes et suscitent identification et rejet. L'humour de Feydeau est à la fois très critique, potentiellement du moins, et très superficiel. Il faut que le public se moque et compatisse à la fois, qu'il y ait un lien entre lui et les personnages.

Ce lien correspond aux nouveaux rapports sociaux qui caractérisent la seconde partie du XIXe siècle, du fait en particulier de l'essor de "couches nouvelles", pour reprendre l'expression de Gambetta. Plusieurs phénomènes concomitants méritent d'être notés. D'une part la France connaît une très forte baisse de natalité. Alors que la population augmente de 29% entre 1801 et 1851, elle n'augmente plus que de 9% entre 1851 et 1901.[19] De plus, l'urbanisation toujours plus lente que dans d'autres pays, s'accélère assez brutalement, surtout à Paris. Paris domine et obsède la société française. A tel point que se répand notamment le mythe de l'exode rural, tandis que celui de la ville-vampire se perpétue. L'instruction s'étant développée, la classe des employés est en plein essor. Enfin, la période 1872-1895 correspond à une crise économique pendant laquelle s'intensifie la lutte pour le maintien ou l'accroissement du niveau de vie. Optimisme et pessimisme se rejoignent sur le plan démographique. La recherche de la réussite sociale s'accorde avec un rétrécissement de la famille afin de donner plus de chances aux enfants. Les difficultés et les inquiétudes aboutissent au même résultat, à part dans les fiefs catholiques. Le mode de vie "bourgeois" s'impose donc irrésistible-ment, du moins dans les villes, et influence même les pauvres.

Il est tentant de faire le rapport avec les indications matérielles de Feydeau. Le décor qu'il décrit correspond presque toujours à un appartement confortable, comportant plusieurs pièces, avec parfois un lavabo visible, un piano, une sonnette, et du mobilier cossu. Les *références* verbales aux problèmes d'hygiène, d'argent, aux mariages intéressants et aux loisirs le confirment. Il y a — c'est presque une loi du genre — des domestiques. Le vaudeville est globalement domestique. Il concerne la vie d'intérieur et exhibe les problèmes en fonction des lieux. Comment refuser de répondre quand on est là? Comment faire croire que l'on est dans sa chambre lorsque l'on découche?[20]

Dans *Un fil à la patte*, les références au progrès sont nombreuses: l'électricité, l'hygiène — le cabinet de toilette joue un rôle important en particulier pour l'acte II, tandis que les dialogues et les gestes reviennent avec insistance sur le fait que l'un des personnages sent mauvais (De Fontanet) — le confort, les loisirs, la presse — au début Bois-d'Enghien empêche les autres de lire l'article du Figaro sur la prestation de Lucette parce qu'ils risquent de lire aussi l'annonce de son mariage... On pourrait multiplier les exemples. De cette façon le vaudeville recoupe les préoccupations générales et les utilise.

L'individu et la société

Or, la question du contrat social et de la démocratisation effective de la société se pose de multiples façons. Elle taraude la société française à la fin du XIXe siècle, à tel point, que la nature et le bien-fondé du rapport entre individus et groupes sont mis en doute.

La représentation de la "vie moderne" porte en fait des tendances, voire des mythes contradictoires. Tout comme il y a un mythe du progrès, il y a un spectre de la décadence; tout comme il y a un engouement pour les thèmes démocratiques, on voit se multiplier les signes d'une peur des masses. La vulgarisation scientifique, en particulier à travers la presse, a contribué à l'implantation d'une conception naturaliste, déterministe de l'individu. A la fin du siècle, on parle d'hérédité, de milieu familial. L'individu est représenté comme le résultat d'une série de causes. On sait que l'effort à la fois médical et médico-légal est pour beaucoup dans cette évolution de l'opinion. On veut savoir quelles raisons font qu'un individu est ou devient un criminel, s'il s'agit d'une "nature" ou d'un conditionnement. Après les médecins, les hygiénistes, voire les juges et les policiers, viennent, notamment, la psychologie sociale et la sociologie. Il est marquant de constater que paraissent à la même époque certains des textes les plus importants de Gabriel Tarde — à la fois juge et promoteur de la psychologie sociale — en 1893 paraît *La logique sociale*; de Gustave Le Bon, sa *Psychologie des foules* date de 1895, et de Durkheim qui écrit *Les règles de la méthode sociologique* en 1894. Cette convergence thématique montre que la problématique du comportement individuel et collectif est centrale à la fin du siècle, dans certains cas obsessionnelle. C'est le même problème pris autrement qui se pose aux théoriciens de l'éducation et de la politique. Pour pouvoir maîtriser et instruire les masses, ou les foules, il faut en comprendre le comportement.

La dénonciation de cette radicalisation positiviste nourrit des courants qui renouent en partie avec le romantisme ou mettent en question l'ensemble du système. Les thèses anarchistes de Jean Grave, qui publie en 1893, *La Société mourante et l'anarchie* puis, en 1895, *La Société future*, sont de ce point de vue significatives. La critique de la société moderne comme rationalisation de la domination par la diffusion du modèle bourgeois, débouche sur un éloge de l'individu rendu à lui-même.[21] Pris sous cet angle le cas de la philosophie de Bergson perd un peu de son mystère. Pour lui aussi, le plus urgent c'est d'explorer la part cachée de l'individu, ce que les mots et les institutions viennent homogénéiser et réduire. A ses yeux d'ailleurs, le vaudeville a plutôt un effet de renforcement. *L'essai sur les données immédiates de la conscience*, publiée en 1889, vise en particulier à montrer l'irréductibilité de la vie de l'esprit par rapport aux outils collectifs, à commencer par le langage, ce dont l'expérience singulière de la durée fournit la preuve.

La vie sociale apparaît donc comme une série de pièges qui préserve le pouvoir d'une minorité. Les classes montantes cherchent à se situer du bon côté, à intégrer le camp de ceux qui profitent du système. Les classes les plus pauvres et les moins instruites subissent et dénoncent, quand elles le peuvent, l'institutionnalisation des inégalités, sous couvert d'idées républicaines. Par ailleurs, des contre-modèles apparaissent ou se précisent: les marginaux, les hors-la-loi — en particulier le truand et la prostituée dont le prestige s'accroît et qui sont représentés à la fois comme les produits d'un système vicieux et l'envers, la négation du bourgeois aussi bien que de ses domestiques — le chemineau qui cumule le prestige de l'indépendance et de la mobilité[22]; et l'artiste qui reprend un peu de ces différents styles de vie.

En somme, le théâtre, avec les moyens qui lui sont propres et des innovations, exhibe et interroge les modèles sociaux dominants, dans une perspective urbaine — en fait même parisienne — et en intégrant l'un des lieux communs du temps, la lutte individuelle pour une situation. Les variations sur la bêtise et le caractère étriqué de la vie bourgeoise sont dédoublées par la conscience de la valeur des garanties qu'elle offre. La peur de l'âge des masses, l'enthousiasme pour les formes du progrès et l'énigme de la personnalité, tissent donc un réseau serré, particulièrement favorable aux mécanismes du vaudeville.

De plus, par un remarquable renversement et un déplacement des fonctions, un théâtre moderne, autonome s'affirme. L'artiste prétend de plus en plus à une reconnaissance interne au monde de l'art, contre les philistins, contre la domination des modes, du goût "bourgeois", des critères quantitatifs — Combien de spectateurs? — contre le pouvoir de la presse qu'il faut utiliser et non subir. Dans tous les cas le bourgeois comme spectre, comme type ou comme devenir sert de point de repère.

L'incipit de *Monsieur Teste*, que Paul Valéry publie en 1896, résume en cela l'inquiétude équivoque des contemporains et la prétention d'une minorité face aux effets de la démocratisation: "La bêtise n'est pas mon fort." dit le narrateur...

Notes

1. A. Jarry, *Oeuvres complètes*, vol.I (Gallimard, Pléiade, 1972), p. 1052, date inconnue.

2. E. Weber, *France, Fin de Siècle* (Harvard University Press, 1986); trad. fr. *Fin de siècle* (Fayard), p. 207.

3. Cf. J. Moréas, 'Un manifeste littéraire, Le Symbolisme', Figaro, 18 sept. 1886, cité par L. Delevoy, in: *Le symbolisme* (Skira, 1982), p. 71.

4. A. Jarry, *Oeuvres complètes*, p. 1053.

5. *Ibidem*, p. 1050.

6. Cf. en particulier, P. Bénichou, *Le sacre de l'écrivain* (Corti, 1973); P. Bourdieu, *Les règles de l'art* (Seuil, 1992).

7. A. Jarry, *Ubu* (Gallimard, 1978), pp. 130-132.

8. Cf. en particulier, S. Faure, *L'Anarchie en cour d'assises*, cité par J. Maitron (dans J. Maitron, *Ravachol et les anarchistes*, Gallimard, 1992), pp. 27-35.

9. O.C., vol. I, pp. 1030-1031. Les questions étaient les suivantes: "1. Un apaisement s'est-il fait dans nos esprits au sujet du traité de Francfort? 2. Pense-t-on moins à l'Alsace-Lorraine, quoique, prenant à rebours le conseil de Gambetta, on en parle toujours autant? 3. Prévoit-on un moment où l'on ne considérerait plus la guerre de 1870-1871 que comme un évènement purement historique? 4. Si une guerre venait à surgir entre les deux nations, trouverait-elle en France, un accueil favorable? Nous vous serions reconnaissants de bien vouloir nous donner, en quelques lignes, sur ces questions: 1. votre opinion personnelle; 2. selon vous l'opinion de la jeunesse; 3. selon vous, l'opinion moyenne du pays."

10. *Ibidem*.

11. Cf. compte rendu du *Journal d'un anarchiste*, d'Augustin Léger, publié en mai 1896 dans le *Mercure de France*, repris dans O.C, vol. I, p. 1012-1013. cf. aussi l'attitude de O. Mirbeau, selon J.F Nivet et P. Michel, *Octave Mirbeau* (Séguier, 1990), chap.XIV.

12. O.C, vol. I, pp. 345-398.

13. Montesquieu, *Lettres persanes*, lettre XI et suivantes.

14. Cf. H. Behar, *Jarry dramaturge* (Nizet, 1980), chap. I.

15. H. Gidel, *Feydeau* (Flammarion, 1991), p. 125.

16. Id. Chap. VII, VIII, IX.

17. Cf. aussi la même année, *La peur des coups* (1894), de Courteline, pour un autre exemple de poltronnerie.

18. Dans ses articles sur le comique publiés en 1899 dans la *Revue de Paris* et regroupés dans *Le rire* (P.U.F, 1940), pp. 77-78. Bergson prend certains de ses exemples chez Labiche. Cf. par exemple chap. I p. 47; chap. II p. 76.

19. Cf. J.P. Rioux, *Chronique d'une fin de siècle, France, 1889-1900* (Seuil, 1991), p. 169. 1801: 27 350 000 hbts; 1851: 35 780 000; 1901: 38 343 000.

20. G. Feydeau, *Tailleur pour dame*, acte I.

21. Cf. aussi M. Stirner, *Der Einzige und sein Eigenthum* (1844).

22. Cf. en particulier J.Richepin, *Le Chemineau* (1897), et les dessins de Steinlen.

Serge Salaün
ZARZUELA ET *CUPLÉ*:
IDENTITÉ NATIONALE ET MÉTISSAGE CULTUREL

Dans les éphémérides de l'année 1894, les oeuvres réellement marquantes pour l'ensemble du théâtre espagnol, celles que la critique retient avec insistance pour leur qualité ou pour la 'recette', sont au nombre de deux qui appartiennent au théâtre lyrique, à la *zarzuela*, et ce n'est pas un hasard. L'année 1894 est vraiment 'lancée', le 17 février, par *La Verbena de la Paloma*, livret de Ricardo de la Vega, musique de Tomás Bretón, un des plus grands succès de l'histoire de la *zarzuela*, et se termine dans l'apothéose (à l'époque la critique ne rechigne pas à la surenchère dithyrambique), le 16 novembre, avec *El Tambor de granaderos*, livret d'Emilio Sánchez Pastor, musique de Ruperto Chapí, une oeuvre qui, pour oubliée qu'elle soit aujourd'hui, n'en est pas moins considérée par les spécialistes comme un des plus grands classiques du genre.

Les auteurs de ces deux oeuvres y exploitent sans états d'âme plusieurs des 'filons' essentiels de la *zarzuela*: le filon populiste (les rues, les bas quartiers et le petit peuple de Madrid dans *La Verbena*), la fibre patriotique (patriotarde même, dans *El Tambor*), la 'matière' verbale et ludique de la langue populaire (ingéniosité et plaisir du mot) et, bien évidemment, le patrimoine musical national qui va des folklores régionaux à la tradition des marches militaires. Le 'cru' 94 paraît donc semblable à celui des années qui précèdent ou qui suivent: on serait tenté de dire qu'il s'agit d'une année tout à fait normale dans le panorama théâtral espagnol des dix dernières années du siècle, avec ses grands succès et ses semi-échecs, une année qui confirme la suprématie du théâtre lyrique court et l'hégémonie d'une scène consacrée au rire, à la légèreté et à une musique bien enracinée dans le patrimoine national. Cette perspective d'un théâtre espagnol replié sur lui-même est bien réelle, mais il conviendra de nuancer, car en 1894, quoique discret, le XXe siècle se profile déjà.

Le monopole du *género chico* (le 'petit genre')

La décennie 1890-1900 constitue certainement la grande époque du 'petit genre' (petit renvoyant ici à la durée: une heure), son apogée si l'on en croit les critiques les plus autorisés (Deleito y Piñuela, Zurita, Valencia[1]). Le *género chico*, né sous des auspices révolutionnaires, dans l'effervescence culturelle et politique de signe libéral qui agite Madrid en 1867-68, est devenu, sous la Restauration monarchique (après 1875), un exceptionnel instrument de captation idéologique entre les mains d'une bourgeoisie en pleine expansion économique et politique. Le *género chico* représente l'entreprise — consciente — de la fraction active de cette bourgeoisie modérée et dynastique, pour regrouper autour d'elle toutes les forces vives de la nation, de l'aristocratie éclairée aux couches populaires, en passant par l'armée. Le *Género chico* est l'instrument de ce *consensus* et le moins que l'on puisse dire est que son succès (culturellement parlant) est allé au-delà de toutes les espérances. Servis par des librettistes de talent tels que Ricardo de la Vega, Celso Lucio, Miguel Ramos Carrión, Javier de Burgos ou Vital Aza, et par des musiciens inspirés et très compétents tels que Barbieri, Arrieta[2], Chapí ou Bretón, la *zarzuela* et, plus généralement, tous les genres courts, avec ou sans musique, ont connu, au cours des années 80 et, surtout, des années 90, un essor foudroyant. A cet égard, il n'est pas exagéré de dire que le 'petit genre' jouit, à la fin du siècle, d'une véritable situation de quasi *monopole théâtral* dans toute l'Espagne. Toutes les autres expressions théâtrales déclinent ou même périclitent comme c'est le cas pour le théâtre national 'classique' et l'opéra (malgré la mode de l'opéra 'vériste' italien et le succès de Wagner dans les dernières années du siècle, pour des publics beaucoup plus 'sélects'): même le *flamenco*, qui a fait vivre des centaines de 'cafés-chantants' pendant la seconde moitié du XIX est en très nette régression.

Même si l'immense majorité des auteurs et compositeurs de *zarzuelas* sont des provinciaux, Barcelone et, surtout, Madrid sont les grands centres de production nationale qui abreuvent tout le pays. La capitale est, en cette fin de siècle, le vrai modèle culturel et de deux façons complémentaires. Madrid, c'est d'abord un filon thématique que la *zarzuela* exploite inlassablement (la rue, la taverne, les tableaux de moeurs, les parlers populaires) et c'est également une façon de consommer, de 'vivre' le théâtre à laquelle adhère le pays tout entier. On n'insistera pas sur sa renommée persistante de ville frivole et sur son penchant pour la vie nocturne (les dernières séances peuvent se prolonger au-delà de 2 heures du matin, malgré les décrets des gouverneurs, et les administrations et commerces n'ouvrent qu'à 11 heures du matin), mais c'est un trait pertinent qui conditionne directement l'histoire culturelle espagnole.

Entre 1894 et 1900, Madrid possède en moyenne 19 théâtres; 11 se consacrent, en tout ou partie, au 'petit genre' (les plus célèbres sont El Eslava et, surtout, El Apolo, pompeusement qualifié de 'cathédrale du petit genre'). Alors que le répertoire dramatique classique n'autorise qu'une séance par soirée, les théâtres du 'petit genre' donnent jusqu'à 6 séances quotidiennes: 2 l'après-midi, pour un public vraisemblablement plus féminin, plus jeune, plus populaire, et 4 le soir, dont la fameuse 'quatrième', très appréciée des noctambules et de la bonne société — masculine, essentiellement. La formule donne de si bons résultats qu'en 1901 le Théâtre Apolo en rajoutera une 7ème.

La demande est donc considérable. Voici une estimation des entrées réalisées par le Théâtre Apolo pour l'année 1900 (une excellente année, il est vrai). L'Apolo peut contenir plus de 2000 personnes, car en dehors des places assises individuelles, le public s'entasse dans les 'baignoires' et les 'loges', sans parler du 'poulailler' ou le public populaire, debout, semble avoir été particulièrement compressé. Il offre 6 'sections' (séances) par jour, ce qui fait une moyenne de 12 000 entrées/jour. Et comme il est ouvert, cette année là, au moins 320 jours[3], on aboutit à un total — prudent — de 3 840 000 entrées.[4]

Si on ajoute toutes les autres salles du 'petit genre' — l'Eslava, par exemple, bien que légèrement plus petit, fonctionne de la même manière et avec un public aussi enthousiaste —, le total des entrées des théâtres de la capitale est probablement supérieur à 12 millions, ce qui représente un score vertigineux pour une ville d'environ 500 000 habitants en 1900, car ce ne sont ni les 'touristes' ni les provinciaux qui constituent le gros de l'affluence.

En province, le phénomène est tout à fait identique. La demande est tout aussi vorace. Le nombre des théâtres ne cesse de croître entre 1840 et la fin du siècle. Toutes les capitales et grandes villes de province ont au moins un ou deux théâtres commerciaux, sans parler des salles d'amateurs ou de sociétés diverses; Malaga, 130 000 habitants vers 1900, dispose d'environ 5000 places disponibles, soit une place de théâtre pour 26 habitants.[5] Même des petites communes de 2000 ou 3000 habitants peuvent posséder une salle de spectacle.[6] Un dernier exemple, celui de Carthagène, 90 000 habitants en 1900, deux grands théâtres dont un se consacre au 'petit genre', avec 4 séances par jour en semaine et 7 les samedis, dimanches et jours fériés; au cours du seul mois de janvier, j'ai répertorié entre 150 et 160 représentations dont 140 pour la seule *zarzuela* (27 titres différents). Dans l'autre théâtre, consacré au répertoire dramatique, même les séances 'sérieuses' sont ponctuées par un 'final' comique sous forme de saynette ou de *fin de fiesta*.

Les nouveautés arrivent dans les provinces ou villes les plus reculées dans les mois ou même les semaines qui suivent la 'première', grâce aux compagnies itinérantes (90 à la fin du siècle selon Sinesio Delgado) ou fixes. Le développement du 'petit genre' se mesure aussi à la prolifération de sociétés (professionnelles, politiques, associatives, etc.) ou de 'troupes' amateurs, dont le répertoire, pour ce que j'en sais, puise essentiellement dans le 'petit genre'. La vogue s'étend aux salons bourgeois de la Péninsule qui donnent des représentations privées.

Les 'saisons théâtrales' de province ne sont pas toujours aussi bien fournies qu'à Malaga ou à Carthagène, mais, les compagnies tournent, se succèdent selon des calendriers plus ou moins bien établis. En 1894, le Théâtre Novedades d'Almeria fait alterner cinq compagnies différentes pendant l'été. Il existe, parallèlement à cette mécanique de la représentation, une *sociabilité* liée au théâtre extrêmement active et variée: périodiques et revues regorgent d'informations sur les oeuvres, sur les déplacements des compagnies et des vedettes, sur l'organisation de banquets et d'hommages. Il faudrait ajouter également toute la sociabilité 'galante' qui accompagne la chose théâtrale, car les actrices et chanteuses sont des mets fort prisés des bourgeois de province. Avec le XXe siècle et avec le développement des cabarets et de la chanson, cette sociabilité augmentera de façon prodigieuse et s'étendra à toutes les couches de la population (masculine, évidemment, pour ce qui est de la galanterie qui, en fait, recouvrira un réseau national de prostitution liée aux spectacles).

Face à une demande d'une telle ampleur, il y a bien sûr un problème d'offre et, très vite, de surenchère. Au cours des dernières années du XIXe siècle, le nombre des auteurs, compositeurs, musiciens augmente considérablement.

Celui des artistes et, tout particulièrement, celui des chanteuses et des danseuses, prend des 'proportions alarmantes' (selon l'auteur de l'éditorial de *El Teatro Español*, nr. 26, 9 juillet 1898), car il est clair que les talents des demoiselles, pour chanter ou réciter, ne sont pas toujours à l'unisson de leurs appas.

Pour satisfaire cette demande exigeante (et de plus en plus intolérante), il faut des oeuvres en abondance. Les grands succès inoubliables sont plus rares que les 'fours' ou les semi-échecs, quels qu'en soient les auteurs. Il est par exemple significatif qu'Isaac Albéniz, qui a fait jouer deux *zarzuelas* en 1894, *San Antonio de la Florida* et *La Sortija*, n'ait reçu qu'un accueil mitigé pour la première (5 représentations en tout) et quasiment glacial pour la seconde, alors que ces deux oeuvres, dans leur version française et anglaise, feront carrière à l'étranger; étonnant paradoxe que la carrière d'Albéniz en grande partie conditionnée par son échec dans la *zarzuela*! La comparaison avec *La Verbena de la Paloma*, qui a occupé deux séances de l'Apolo par jour jusqu'en 1895, devant des salles pleines, est révélateur du fonctionnement du système.[7] En 1894, l'Apolo, d'après mes estimations, ne 'crée' que 13 oeuvres nouvelles, pour 22 reprises, mais *La Verbena* remplit bien les caisses.

Pour alimenter ce théâtre boulimique, tous les moyens sont bons. On exploite des filons régionaux (Madrid, l'Andalousie, l'Aragon), ou des filons thématiques (une oeuvre qui a bien marché suscite des 'suites': avec *La fiesta de San Antón*, par exemple, Arniches profite des retombées de *El santo de la Isidra*), on plagie à tour de bras le répertoire français du boulevard ou les auteurs à la mode (Feuillet, Hennequin, Scribe plus que tout autre: *Los dioses del Olimpo*, d'Arderius, en février 1894, rappelle de très près *Orphée aux enfers*, d'Offenbach), on parodie des oeuvres à succès (en mars 94, *Los maestros cantaores* sont une parodie des *Maîtres chanteurs* de Wagner). D'après Zurita, plus de 1500 *zarzuelas* ont été créées entre 1890 et 1900, ce qui donne une moyenne de 150 par an: on fera encore mieux par la suite. La qualité moyenne des oeuvres représentées en pâtit évidemment beaucoup, surtout que la nouvelle génération de librettistes n'a pas le talent de la précédente: et le public n'est guère tendre.

La situation en ce fin de siècle est donc paradoxale. Il y a une situation d'inflation en ce qui concerne les théâtres, les auteurs, les compositeurs, les artistes. Le public est bien là, partout, toutes classes sociales confondues, solidement enraciné dans un patrimoine musical et textuel qui ne cesse de s'enrichir. Evidemment, la quantité s'implique pas la qualité, mais elle ne l'exclut pas non plus: des dizaines d'oeuvres excellentes verront encore le jour. Dès 1894-95, surgissent dans la presse des cris d'alarme, des analyses de ce que l'on nomme déjà la 'décadence' du théâtre espagnol et qui stigmatisent le manque de professionalisme des uns et des autres, les causes et les responsables de cette inflation galopante qui débouche sur des recettes, des stéréotypes usés jusqu'à la corde. Mais ce concept de 'crise' qui sera le *leit-motiv* de toute la critique théâtrale jusqu'en 1936, inlassablement ressassé et décliné sous tous ses aspects, ne doit pourtant pas faire oublier que la *zarzuela* et le 'petit genre', sous leurs modalités les plus variées, sont un phénomène culturel de masses, et le resteront pratiquement jusqu'en 1936, malgré la concurrence de nouveaux spectacles et de nouvelles formules théâtrales. Le type de théâtre qui se consolide entre 1890 et 1900 autour des genres courts, avec ou sans musique, avec ses modes de consommation et ses sociabilités, fait figure de monument, un monument vivant auquel s'identifie une grande partie du pays, de quelque catégorie sociale ou professionnelle que ce soit. Il constitue aussi un patrimoine de référence diversifié, apte à participer à de multiples manifestations de la vie publique ou privée qui va des orphéons, *bandas*, orchestres, chanteurs des rues, pianos mécaniques, aux pratiques plus individuelles ou familiales.

L'émergence de la modernité

La solidité du monopole de la *zarzuela* et du 'petit genre', leur indiscutable popularité, opposent, dans un premier temps, un obstacle décisif à la pénétration des modes et des spectacles nouveaux qui ont cours en Europe. On serait tenté d'analyser ce monument théâtral espagnol en termes de 'résistance', de refus de la culture étrangère, de repli sur des valeurs autochtones; la fin du siècle, avec les désastres militaires et politiques, les crises multiples qui affectent la société espagnole, inviterait à privilégier cette perspective du repli sur soi. Ce n'est pas tout à fait faux, mais la réalité exige la nuance.

C'est vrai que la *zarzuela* a bâti son succès sur des décors et des thématiques populaires (ou populistes), sur un univers de petits métiers, de rues et de places qui renvoient à une société pré-capitaliste, artisanale, donc déjà archaïque à la charnière des deux siècles, soudée autour de valeurs patrioti-ques et morales destinées à protéger une hispanité menacée dans toutes ses intégrités. C'est vrai, également, que la *zarzuela* a contribué lourdement à propager dans le pays un sentiment guerrier et chauvin qui allait dans le sens de la politique catastrophique menée par le gouvernement (et la monarchie) contre les indépendantistes cubains, contre les Etats-Unis (alliés des Cubains); le nombre très élevé de *zarzuelas* patriotardes qui exaltaient l'armée, du brave petit soldat espagnol à l'héroïque officier en passant par le retour au pays du soldat blessé ou infirme, au son de l'inévitable marche militaire destinée à 'chauffer' le public, revèle bien une volonté de légitima-tion et de sensibilisation. Le cas de *El tambor de granaderos*, en 1894, en est une belle illustration: à partir de la référence — glorieuse, évidemment — à la lutte anti-napoléonnienne et à la 'Guerre d'Indépendance', l'histoire de ce jeune tambour qui refuse de prêter serment au drapeau de l'occupant s'inscrit bien dans un projet politique qui se prétend national et collectif. La *zarzuela* qui a pu apparaître quelque fois comme une soupape de contestation s'est définitivement et majoritairement alignée sur l'idéologie des autorités en place. Pour tout dire, la *zarzuela* et le 'petit genre', qui s'évertuent à confondre public et peuple, sont bien l'organe d'expression et de transmission des groupes dominants de l'époque qui ne se caractérisent pas par des mesures ou des préoccupations particulièrement sociales. Les éléments les plus populaires commenceront d'ailleurs à déserter les théâtres 'bourgeois' et à bouder la *zarzuela*, précisément à partir de 1900.

L'enracinement de la *Zarzuela* dans le patrimoine culturel national ne s'explique pourtant pas pour des raisons idéologiques. Le public, même le plus populaire, aime qu'on lui raconte de belles histoires, glorieuses ou humbles, qui finissent toujours bien, mais il n'est pas sûr que l'adhésion politique accompagne cette consommation. On a beaucoup insisté sur l'image, le 'reflet' que ce théâtre renvoyait aux masses: le 'peuple' — dit la critique traditionnelle — venait se voir sur scène, dans ses activités et ses propos de tous les jours. Possible! En dépassant cette forte dose de paternalisme qui pèse depuis toujours sur cette culture, il me semble que la raison la plus convaincante de l'adhésion aux valeurs proprement hispaniques, bien plus que par l'effet miroir, s'explique par les supports musicaux qui ont décidé du succès de l'immense majorité des oeuvres.

En fait, c'est presque toujours la musique qui l'emporte. Et, sur ce plan, la *zarzuela* a su récupérer et exalter, dans toute l'Espagne, le patrimoine musical régional et/ou folklorique, dignifié, stylisé si l'on veut, ou réécrit par des compositeurs très talentueux. Ce patrimoine a été diffusé et consommé sans ostracisme, chaque région aimant se retrouver dans l'image stéréotypée que la *zarzuela* lui renvoie, tout en appréciant les patrimoines des autres régions. Ainsi la *jota*, danse aragonaise, a-t-elle pu devenir le symbole des valeurs nationales; ainsi la séguedille castillane, et les musiques andalouses émaillent-elles systématiquement les partitions de *zarzuelas*, en alternance fort diplomatique (la *soleá* de *La Verbena*, jouée sur un bastringue de café-chantant madrilène en est un des plus beaux exemples). Il est bien évident que la *zarzuela* offre un catalogue de rythmes et de références culturelles parfaitement intégrées dans l'actualité du spectateur, dans son présent; un patrimoine vivant qui n'est pas perçu comme archaïque ni même folklorique.

Mais toutes les 'résistances', naturelles ou favorisées par les groupes dirigeants, que l'on peut attribuer à la *zarzuela*, ne pouvaient indéfiniment s'opposer à la pénétration en Espagne des spectacles et des modalités théâtrales qui sont à la mode en France, en Allemagne ou en Angleterre depuis plusieurs décennies déjà. Sur ce point, l'Espagne est en retard, un retard qu'elle va combler... grâce à la *zarzuela*, paradoxalement. C'est en effet, au coeur même du monument national que la modernité européenne fera son apparition, en investissant ce qui a fait son succès depuis ses débuts: la musique et les chanteuses.

Les charmes des artistes féminines, sur scène, sont un puissant adjuvant du succès, en Espagne comme ailleurs, et plus encore dans les genres comiques ou légers. Les chanteuses de *zarzuelas* n'échappent pas à la règle et c'est même là un filon que les auteurs ont exploité sans vergogne depuis le début (la *tonadillera* du XVIIIe siècle avait déjà mauvaise réputation et *El joven Telémaco*, en 1866, avait popularisé la *suripanta*, l'ancêtre de la *tiple* point trop farouche). Dans la dernière décennie du XIXe qui provoque une inflation des oeuvres et des interprètes, la plastique de telle ou telle actrice devient un 'argument de vente' tout à fait admis. En 1891, une actrice de *El monaguillo* (l'Enfant de choeur) déchaîne la frénésie des spectateurs en chantant son aria juchée sur un âne et montrant un peu de cheville.

L'évolution, sur ce point, est nette et irréversible. Les pièces *picantes* (osées) se multiplient. Certains théâtres se spécialisent dans ce nouveau 'genre' théâtral qui s'avère particulièrement rentable, ce qui fait qu'on le retrouve très vite sur la plupart des scènes du 'petit genre'. En province, cela fera fureur, et très durablement. En 1894, par exemple, la presse signale les mérites suggestifs de plusieurs pièces en termes sans équivoque: *La Bayadera o la bella Chiquita*, *El chaleco blanco* (zarzuela tout à fait décente, mais avec un orphéon féminin), *Los dioses del Olimpo*, parodie d'Offenbach, dont l'attrait le plus vanté est d'ordre 'plastique' (le journaliste invite à y admirer les 'mollets' des demoiselles: "Aquello es una verdadera exposición de piernas, capaz de hacer pecar a un santo".[8]).

De 1893-94 à 1910, c'est le règne de ce qu'on a appelé en Espagne le *género ínfimo* (le 'genre infime') et la *Sicalipsis*, un néologisme de plus qui désigne, au départ, la pornographie ou l'érotisme scénique. Et il est vrai qu'en matière d'érotisme théâtral, l'Espagne austère fait des progrès très rapides. A la fin du siècle, la revue *Juan Rana* invente même le *decenzómetro* ('appareil qui indique les degrés de décence des spectacles de la capitale'): l'échelle va de + 40 pour le très aristocratique (et peu fréquenté) Théâtre Royal, à -30 pour le San Juan de Dios.[9]

Parallèlement à cette invasion d'un érotisme plus ou moins hardi (mais qui le deviendra), on assiste à la timide pénétration en Espagne de la chanson de Variétés et du *Music-hall*. C'est en 1893, au Théâtre Barbieri, que l'on fixe, pour l'Espagne, l'apparition sur scène d'une chanteuse et d'un 'tour de chant'. Augusta Bergès, une allemande, y interprétait *La Pulga*, une polka d'origine française ou italienne, au cours de laquelle l'innocente héroïne se livrait à une frénétique chasse à la puce sur son opulente (et peu vêtue) personne. La chanson a alimenté le répertoire de centaines de chanteuses jusqu'en 1925, au moins[10], ce qui donne une idée de son succès auprès du public péninsulaire.

Le public s'est lassé des intrigues insipides et répétitives, il veut des "divettes"[11] appétissantes et des chansons qui lui collent à la mémoire et se détourne des théâtres traditionnels dès qu'il comprend qu'il peut avoir le même spectacle (chair et musique), pour bien moins cher, et de bien plus près, dans des salles spécialisées. Et ce, d'autant plus que le confort des théâtres a fait de gros progrès en Espagne en cette fin de siècle: le chauffage semble bien maîtrisé et, dès 1892-93, l'électricité se répand dans les lieux de spectacles; ce sont d'ailleurs les cabarets et les cafés-chantants qui en tireront immédiatement le plus grand profit, pour le confort et pour la 'mise en scène' artistique. La frivolité, par le biais de la nécessité commerciale, est un des moteurs du progrès. Le succès du *Music-hall*, du 'cabaret' ou du 'café concert' est vite assuré, surtout dans la mesure où ils s'ouvrent à des publics nouveaux, les couches populaires (et les femmes, après 1912) en particulier qui, auparavant, étaient plutôt exclues de la pratique des spectacles et de toute la sociabilité qui s'y rapporte.

Entre 1894 et 1900, tout porte à croire que les progrès de cette modernité sont assez lents. Ce que l'on voit surtout, c'est que le 'petit genre' fait de la résistance: en accueillant les musiques à la mode venues de l'étranger (la fin du siècle coincide avec l'essor de la polka, de la mazurka, de la valse et du très 'madrilène' *chotis*, qui, comme on sait, vient de la *scottish*), et entrant dans la spirale de la *sicalipsis*. Le nombre de cabarets ou de salles spécialement adaptées au *Music-hall* est encore limité[12] et leur apparition est commentée par la presse. En 1894, le premier *Music-hall* espagnol, administré par un Français et hébergé dans le Théâtre Moderne de Madrid, est ainsi présenté par *El Teatro moderno* (nr. 24, 9-8-1894): "Une société, que l'on prétend française, en a pris la responsabilité pour exploiter un spectacle semblable à celui des *Folies Bergères* de Paris. Il y aura une salle de lecture de la presse, un restaurant, un théâtre et autres divertissements" (le jeu en est exclu). En 1900, l'ouverture du Salon Japonais, le cabaret le plus luxueux d'Espagne, fait beaucoup parler de lui, surtout quand le Gouverneur en ordonne la fermeture après le premier soir, toujours pour cause de *sicalipsis*. Mais il semble quand même que le *Music-hall* et la chanson de variété, qui deviendra très vite *el cuplé*, se soient répandus en Espagne, discrètement mais sûrement, dans les théâtres eux-mêmes.[13]

J'observe, dans les programmations des divers théâtres de Madrid ou de province, que des 'compagnies mixtes'[14] et bientôt, des danseuses ou des chanteuses en soliste, occupent une séance complète (une heure). Ici, c'est un orchestre de six chiens qui tient la vedette, là c'est un illusionniste. Le Gouverneur de Madrid, en 1895, interdit un spectacle d'hypnotiseurs dans les Cirques Colón et Parish. Ce qui est très à la mode, dans tout le pays, c'est la 'danse serpentine' où s'illustrent de belles — fausses ou vraies — étrangères (Marbelle, Géraldine, Ida Fuller, en 1894 et 1895).

1894 marque également les débuts espagnols, au Théâtre Principal puis au Granvía, de Frégoli qui reviendra en vedette à l'Apolo en 1895 où il occupera deux séances: lors de son 'bénéfice' d'adieu, il incarnera 50 personnages et effectuera 80 transformations. Pour ce qui est des chanteuses, les programmes sont encore discrets. On sait que Mistinguett et Nitta Jo — celle qui a popularisé le *Tararaboum dihé*, chanson 'épileptique'— se sont produits à Barcelone, la province la plus ouverte aux influences étrangères (et dont on sait peu de choses). En décembre 1894, La Patti et la Nicolini séduisent Valence et Almeria; leurs cachets parisiens font rêver les folliculaires espagnols (33 000 et 22 000 francs par soirée, respectivement). En janvier 1897, une chanteuse française, Mlle Blanche Liscaut, occupe une séance à l'Apolo, mais le public n'apprécie que modérément sa gouaille et son accent parisien.

En fait, avant la fin du siècle, les théâtres spécialisés dans le 'petit genre', qui commencent eux aussi à avoir des problèmes de gestion et de trésorerie malgré l'affluence, ouvrent de plus en plus leurs portes à des spectacles qui n'y ont pas leur place et qui les quitteront dès qu'ils le pourront. L'exemple du cinéma complète ce qui vient d'être dit. La première séance de cinémato-graphe a eu lieu au Théâtre Apolo, en 1896.[15] Il n'est pas rare, dans les années suivantes, de voir les théâtres, petits ou grands, consacrer un entracte ou une séance entière, à des projections de cinéma, toujours pour garder ce public populaire qui a tendance à chercher ailleurs des plaisirs vifs et renouvelés. L'extrordinaire prolifération des cabarets ou cafés avec orchestre et spectacle, à partir de 1900, marque indiscutablement un tournant.

Au fond, si l'on ne s'en tient qu'à l'année 1894 ou à celles qui l'entourent, et qui sont souvent présentées comme des années 'ordinaires', le panorama théâtral espagnol apparaît quand même doté d'une indéniable originalité. D'une part, il oppose à l'effervescente modernité européenne le barrage efficace de milliers d'oeuvres quelque peu crispées sur leur spécificité hispanique; c'est la célébration du *casticismo*, de *lo castizo*[16], censé représenter les valeurs culturelles et identitaires inaltérables, la communauté tout entière jouant et se voyant jouer sur le mode de la fête et du plaisir. Que l'histoire et la société infligent de cinglants démentis à un panorama aussi idyllique, c'est une évidence, et pourtant la *zarzuela* et tous les genres courts garderont leurs adeptes (après tout, la chanson n'est que le court comme unité de consommation culturelle poussée à l'extrême). Le fait que l'on traduise ou que l'on joue fort peu de *zarzuelas* hors d'Espagne confirmerait ce côté autarcique de la scène espagnole. Mais il faut reconnaître qu'elle constitue un patrimoine exceptionnel, avec des oeuvres, pour méconnues qu'elles soient, dont la qualité est indiscutable.

D'autre part, l'Espagne, toujours plus soucieuse de modernité qu'il n'y paraît, ne demande qu'à s'ouvrir. Et c'est le théâtre 'mineur', 'populaire', celui qui, en principe, devrait s'opposer à toute évolution, qui favorise les influences étrangères, même si c'est pour des fins commerciales. Il l'a d'ailleurs toujours fait, en s'inspirant d'Offenbach, des Bouffes Parisiens, des Revues de fin d'année, en hispanisant, en 'digérant' les rythmes venus du nord, comme il assimilera les rythmes anglo-saxons et les rythmes 'tropicaux' au tournant du siècle. A bien y regarder, le *casticismo* espagnol est teinté de métissage. Et l'idée communément admise d'un retard espagnol, en cette fin de siècle, serait à nuancer. Bien sûr, en 1900, l'Espagne est loin d'avoir autant de salles de spectacle, toutes catégories réunies, que la France, l'Allemagne ou le Royaume Uni[17], mais, au cours des années 1910 et 1920, elle les dépassera allègrement. La véritable originalité de l'Espagne c'est que le matériau local et national ne cesse jamais vraiment d'être opératoire et que la modernité, pour être vraiment moderne, a besoin de garder ses racines ancrées dans le terreau de la tradition.

Notes

1. José Deleito y Piñuela, *Origen y apogeo del género chico* (Madrid: Revista de Ocidente, 1949), Antonio Valencia, *El género chico. Antología de textos completos* (Madrid: Taurus, 1962), Marciano Zurita, *Historia del género chico* (Madrid: Prensa Popular, 1920).

2. Ces deux compositeurs prestigieux meurent en février 94; Barbieri le jour de la 'première' de *La Verbena*.

3. Il est fermé entre le 5 août et le 2 septembre, ainsi que 3 jours à Pâques. Par prudence, j'ai supposé que quelques séances ou jours ont pu servir pour les répétitions qui étaient, à l'époque, très brèves; on connaît le cas d'une œuvre livrée aux acteurs à 11 heures du matin pour être jouée à 8 heures le soir!

4. Cette estimation est déduite des informations fournies par 'Chispero' (Víctor Ruiz Albéniz), *Teatro Apolo. Historial, anecdotario y estampas madrileñas de su tiempo (1873-1929)* (Madrid: Prensa Castellana, 1953).

5. En 1908, les théâtres de Malaga donnent plus de 1130 représentations qui correspondent à plus de 320 titres différents.

6. Dans le Campo de Cartagena, un bourg (500 habitants au début du siècle) a conservé son 'théâtre' de 200 places.

7. Ceci dit, je ne suis pas sûr que la musique de *La Verbena* soit inférieure aux *zarzuelas* d'Albéniz.

8. *El Teatro moderno*, nr. 1 (17-2-94).

9. Le théâtre des Variétés est coté à -15; quant à l'Apolo, qui cherche lui aussi à retenir la clientèle par tous les moyens, il est coté à +8. Quand on connaît l'opinion de nombreux critiques sur l'indécence qui envahit l'Apolo, on n'ose imaginer le spectacle offert sur les planches du San Juan de Dios.

10. Javier Barreiro affirme qu'une Espagnole, Sofía Alvera, l'aurait devancée, mais en moins lascif: *Raquel Meller y su tiempo* (Zaragoza: Diputación General de Aragón), 1992, p. 21.

11. Un mot typique de l'époque qui voit également évoluer le sens du mot *tiple* de soprano à 'cocotte'.

12. On utilise apparemment les 'Cirques' (théâtres ronds), nombreux en Espagne au XIXe siècle, adaptés plus spécialement aux spectacles équestres, très prisés semble-t-il (un domaine fort peu étudié).

13. Pour les cabarets et leur programmation, la presse est plus discrète, pour ne pas dire muette, en ce qui concerne les établissements qui ne sont pas de haut de gamme.

14. Nom que l'on donnait à des troupes qui offraient différents numéros de variétés: équilibristes, prestidigitateurs, 'transformistes'...

15. Dans les années précédentes, toutes sortes d'expériences, avec des appareils et des spectacles insolites, annonçaient la naissance du cinéma.

16. Ces mots qui, selon les dictionnaires renvoient à quelque chose 'd'authentique' et même de 'pur', sont dérivés de *casta* (caste).

17. Angleterre; 580 théâtres en 1899, 150 000 personnes employées pour un total de 500 000 entrées par jour. Pour l'ensemble du Royaume Uni, Les chiffres s'élèvent à 3000 théâtres, 850 000 employés, 1 250 000 entrées/jour (source: *El Nuevo Fígaro*, Madrid, nr. 729, 30-11-1899).
Allemagne, en 1900: 270 théâtres, 380 salles de 'variétés', 1650 salles de concert, 1500 cafés-concerts, 5800 salles pour 'audition', 273 éditeurs de musique (à titre de comparaison, à cette époque, l'Espagne en a 3), 1800 'négociants en musique', 33 'maisons d'enregistrement', etc. La profession occupe 1 500 000 personnes (source: *El Mundo artístico musical*, Madrid, nr. 3 du 30-5-1900).

Margot Versteeg
1894: *LA VERBENA DE LA PALOMA*, PROTOTYPE DE LA SAYNÈTE MADRILÈNE

De nouvelles modalités intéressantes se présentent aux alentours de 1894 dans le théâtre lyrique espagnol. Notamment l'avenir du 'genre infime' et des variétés s'annonce prometteur. L'apparition de ces nouvelles tendances n'empêche pourtant pas qu'à la fin du XIXe siècle le *género chico* (c'est-à-dire, le 'petit genre') maintienne une place prépondérante, et, qui plus est, jouisse d'une situation de quasi monopole dans la vie théâtrale espagnole, que le théâtre disons 'conventionnel' n'arrive plus à animer. Ainsi au cours des dix dernières années du XIXe siècle, en pleine apogée du petit genre, Madrid compte onze théâtres (Deleito 1949: 182), sur un total de dix-neuf établissements, qui se consacrent, en permanence ou en été seulement, aux représentations dites 'par heure'. Les représentations par heure sont des représentations indépendantes, d'une heure chacune, dans lesquelles sont représentées les pièces en un acte qui constituent le répertoire du petit genre. Plus de 1500 pièces seraient passées en première au cours des dix dernières années du XIXe siècle (*ibidem*). Ce sont bien les années des succès foudroyants. Si l'on consulte l'anthologie de Antonio Valencia (1962), dans lequel ne figurent que les vrais sommets du genre, il s'avère que les pièces recueillies proviennent pour la plupart de cette période.[1] Plus particulièrement, au cours de l'année 1894, l'année qui nous intéresse ici, ont eu lieu deux premières impressionantes. A partir du 16 novembre 1894, la *zarzuela* comique *El tambor de granaderos*, avec livret de Sánchez Pastor et musique de Ruperto Chapí, fait salle comble dans le théâtre madrilène Eslava. Bien plus grand est le succès de *La verbena de la Paloma*, avec livret de Ricardo de la Vega et musique de Tomás Bretón, dont la première a eu lieu le 17 février de la même année dans l'élégant théâtre Apolo, la fameuse 'cathédrale' du petit genre.[2]
La verbena de la Paloma est une saynète. La saynète est une des modalités du petit genre, tout comme la *zarzuela*, le *juguete*, la revue, et quelques autres sous-genres. A la fin du XIXe siècle la saynète est une petite pièce comique, dont l'action se déroule dans une ambiance urbaine, madrilène, que les pièces ont coutume d'exalter et d'embellir. Les protagonistes sont des personnages populaires qui ont la langue bien pendue et chez qui est surtout soulignée la condition 'plébéienne' (Garrido Gallardo 1983). Les pièces sont normalement pourvues de quelques numéros musicaux, qui en général en déterminent le succès. Les saynètes ont pris a partir des années soixante-dix, une place considérable dans la production entière du petit genre. Ainsi se produisent, au cours des premières années du genre, des *remakes* de saynètes de Don Ramón de la Cruz du XVIIIe siècle.[3] Et Ricardo de la Vega ne donne-t-il pas lui-même en 1880, c'est-à-dire une quinzaine d'années avant *La verbena de la Paloma*, avec *La canción de la Lola* le départ pour un vrai déluge de saynètes d'intrigue amoureuse? A partir de ce moment-là, les *chulos* et *chulas* madrilènes ne quittent plus les saynètes.[4] Et ils peuplent non pas seulement

les saynètes, mais aussi les autres modalités, puisque le petit genre se caractérise par sa perméabilité: toutes les modalités s'approprient avidement les éléments à succès. C'est là qu'intervient l'aspect commercial.

Il est clair qu'en 1894 une saynète comme *La verbena de la Paloma* ne tombe pas du ciel. Ce n'est pas quelque chose de radicalement neuf, et pas non plus le terme d'un développement. Ricardo de la Vega atteint cependant avec *La verbena de la Paloma* un très haut degré de perfection dans le genre. Par rapport à *La verbena de la Paloma* les personnages de *La canción de la Lola* aparaissent médiocres. Et les saynètes après *La verbena de la Paloma* suivent toujours le même schéma, bien que dans les meilleurs cas avec la variation désirable. Ainsi López Silva souligne dans *La revoltosa* l'effet théâtral de la bourle, et Carlos Arniches va dans *El santo de la Isidra* à l'encontre de l'histoire extrêmement conventionnelle et des personnages très théâtraux en faisant ressortir le langage ludique de ces derniers. Il ne paraît donc pas exageré de qualifier *La verbena de la Paloma* de prototype de la saynète madrilène du XIXe siècle.

La verbena de la Paloma doit surtout son succès à l'excellente partition de Bretón. C'est hors de doute. En ce qui concerne le livret, à mon avis le succès ne se doit pas tant à son originalité qu'à son caractère stéréotypé. C'est un fait que Ricardo de la Vega est un véritable maître dans l'élaboration du typique, ou, soyons méchants et disons plutôt de l'élaboration efficace du stéréotype et du cliché. Je rappelle que la particularité du cliché par rapport au stéréotype tient au fait que le cliché est à l'origine un effet de style (Amossy 1982: 10).

L'usage de clichés et de stéréotypes n'est pas étranger au petit genre. Alors que la Littérature avec une majuscule cherche à éviter le tout fait, le petit genre, lui, est écrit pour être consommé massivement, et n'hésite pas à envoûter le spectateur grâce à des recettes qui ont fait leur preuves.

L'insertion de clichés et de stéréotypes est un procédé intertextuel. Ricardo de la Vega y a recours de deux façons. Ainsi, il utilise des éléments tout faits de la tradition dramatique. C'est à ces éléments que la pièce doit en grande partie son effet comique. Les clichés et stéréotypes empruntés à la vie de tous les jours jouent à leur tour un rôle bien plus dominant. Ils renvoient l'oeuvre à son contexte social. On pourrait dire que les images stéréotypées et les clichés verbaux constituent le patrimoine de la communauté et portent ainsi la marque du social. Avec un discours social Ricardo de la Vega emprunte également le système de valeurs dont ce discours est porteur. Il est donc très intéressant d'étudier la stratégie discursive de *La verbena de la Paloma*, afin de voir le choix et l'utilisation que Ricardo de la Vega effectue des clichés. On verra ainsi comment l'oeuvre se tisse en intégrant dans sa trame un discours social stéréotypé, qui prend appui sur des valeurs que l'on considère communément partagées (Amossy 1982: 29).

Les images stéréotypées et les clichés verbaux comme éléments intertextuels interviennent à divers niveaux de l'oeuvre. Ces niveaux, étroitement imbriqués, sont notamment ceux de la représentation et de l'argumentation.

En outre, les clichés et la stéréotypie interviennent au niveau de l'expression personnelle et — mais très peu — sur le plan du ludique.

Commençons par l'histoire. L'histoire representée dans *La verbena de la Paloma* est aussi divertissante que banale, dans la mesure où elle obéit au schéma préétabli de nombreuses saynètes: c'est l'histoire de la femme qui, par coquetterie ou afin de rendre jaloux son fiancé, flirte avec un tiers. Chez les spectateurs contemporains, ce type d'histoire doit sans doute avoir suscité une réaction de déjà-vu; ils doivent l'avoir tout de suite assimilée aux autres pièces du genre, et aussi l'avoir reconnue comme étant une 'tranche de vie', dans laquelle ils auraient facilement pu être impliqués eux-mêmes. Il est de fait que tout tourne autour de concepts aussi élémentaires que l'amour, la jalousie, l'honneur. L'histoire se résume de la façon suivante. Julián, fils du peuple et franc comme l'or, est au désespoir parce qu'il a vu sa petite amie, la belle et coquette Susana, en compagnie d'un autre homme. Afin de le distraire, sa mère adoptive, la señá Rita, l'entraîne à la populaire fête madrilène de la Paloma, célébrée la veille du 15 aout. Il va de soi que Julián y voit sa Susana qui est avec sa soeur et sa tante hystérique, et se laisse courtiser par le riche et vieux pharmacien Don Hilarión. Au comble de l'indignation, Julián exige les explications de Susana, et c'est le célèbre "¿Dónde vas con mantón de manila?". La mère adoptive apaise Julián, mais celui-ci ne renonce pas. Pendant le bal il déclenche une dispute véhémente qui a pour résultat que le pharmacien bat en retraite, que la tante Antonia est emmenée par la police et que Susana revient à l'amour de Julián. L'histoire ne pourrait être plus simpliste.

L'histoire est aussi banale que les personnages sont stéréotypés et d'ailleurs très réussis — je n'ai rien à dire à ce sujet. Il convient de distinguer ici deux groupes de personnages: ceux qui ont l'air d'être sortis tout droit de la réalité, et ceux que Vega emprunte à la tradition dramatique. Parmi les personnages du premier groupe, les personnages disons 'réalistes', on compte évidemment Julián, Susana, et les parents adoptifs de Julián, la señá Rita et son mari, le cafetier. Si l'on en croit les critiques, ces gens *pauvres mais honnêtes* (faites attention à ces deux termes) auraient pullulé dans certains quartiers de Madrid à la fin du siècle dernier. Les personnages du deuxième groupe se présentent bien différemment. Ils correspondent aussi à des stéréotypes. Ceux-ci ne sont cependant pas reconnus sur la base d'un code primaire telle la réalité, mais sur la base d'un code secundaire telle la tradition dramatique comico-grotesque. Des personnages vicieux comme la celestinesque tante Antonia et le pharmacien coureur de jupons Don Hilarión ont l'air d'être sortis tout droit d'une farce primitive.

Non seulement les figures correspondent à des stéréotypes, mais leur distribution actantielle en clans antagonistes de 'bons' et de 'méchants' est également très stéréotypée. Selon le schéma manichéen vulgarisé à l'époque par le mélodrame, nos personnages pauvres mais honnêtes, défenseurs de la vertu et de l'innocence et représentés dans la pièce de manière 'réaliste', triomphent toujours des vicieux personnages comico-grotesques. En traitant ces derniers invariablement de méchants, on leur assigne un rôle très limité (ils sont là pour produire un effet comique et pour le contraste avec les personnages 'réalistes'); on ridiculise leur vitalité et on neutralise pour ainsi dire leur éventuel pouvoir transgressif.

Dans *La verbena de la Paloma* Ricardo de la Vega s'efforce de faire parler à ses personnages un 'langage populaire madrilène' immédiatement reconnaissable comme tel par les spectateurs. A l'heure de capter ce langage, l'insertion de clichés (ici au sens strict de figures de style usées) joue un rôle important. L'usage de clichés produit l'impression d'un discours transparent et naturel, qui contribue à la vraisemblance des personnages. C'est pourquoi on trouve dans *La verbena de la Paloma*, outre des caractéristiques phonétiques, des locutions sorties du langage populaire. Elles sont à la base du bavardage dépourvu de tout sens du cafetier, que son personnel écoute bouche bée; à la base aussi des ragots politiques qu'échangent les deux policiers, et des propos tenus entre l'indigné Julián et sa hautaine Susana... Mais à part ça, la pièce contient un certain nombre de néologismes, que le peuple madrilène aurait très bien pu utiliser. J'écris expressément 'aurait pu', puisqu'il est évidemment très difficile de retrouver si des expressions comme 'hay que distinguir', 'hoy las ciencias adelantan que es una barbaridad', et 'la mujer no se cría en pañales' sont des expressions inventées, ou si Ricardo de la Vega, qui passe pour un observateur fidèle, les a effectivement enrégistrées quelque part. Même le grand critique catalan Yxart se déclare dans l'impossibilité de se prononcer à ce sujet (Yxart 1987: 107), donc je me trouve en bonne compagnie. Mais il s'avère que Vega a fait preuve d'une grande perspicacité pour le parler populaire dans la mesure où de nombreuses locutions utilisées par lui dans *La verbena de la Paloma* ont plus tard, du fait de l'interaction scène-salle, réussi à occuper une place dans le langage populaire et y circulent comme des clichés. C'est ici le point fort de Ricardo de la Vega. Comme il a du flair pour les locutions populaires, son oeuvre conserve toujours une certaine fraîcheur et une certaine spontanéité, et n'a jamais la banalité qui caractérise les pièces de beaucoup de ses épigones.

Il se produit même dans quelques cas un déraillement ludique du cliché. Je fais allusion à la répétition interminable de la locution 'que tiés madre' par la mère adoptive et la réponse non moins répétitive 'ya lo sé' par son fils. Cependant, Arniches et sa 'tragédie grotesque' sont encore loins.

Vega met des clichés de la vie de tous les jours dans les moules d'expression stéréotypées de la tradition dramatique. Pensons à la façon mélodramatique et sentimentale — très peu réaliste — avec laquelle Julián exprime ses sentiments. Cela vaut d'autant plus pour les personnages comico-grotesques: il y a le latin macaronique du pharmacien et la bordée d'injures carnavalesques de la tante Antonia. La saynète est bel et bien une 'fête du langage'.

Les clichés et les stéréotypes produisent chez les spectateurs un effet de familiarité et de reconnaissance. Ils jouent aussi un rôle au niveau de l'argumentation de l'oeuvre.

Derrière les clichés dans le texte se cachent les lieux communs de la société qui les fait circuler. Plus un cliché est connu et accepté, plus il se trouve assuré de l'appui des spectateurs. Et cela est conforme au but de toutes les pièces du petit genre, qui est d'être consommé massivement. De par les clichés l'oeuvre se réfère à un discours social considéré comme partagé. Si dans *La verbena de la Paloma* des locutions comme 'también la gente de pueblo tiene su corazoncito' réussissent à enthousiasmer des milliers de spectateurs, c'est précisément parce qu'elles expriment les valeurs du contexte socio-culturel dont elles font partie. Des valeurs, bien sûr, que les producteurs des pièces aiment propager.

Le décor typique des saynètes remplit une fonction analogue au cliché. D'une part il favorise la reconnaissance de la situation représentée et il permet de l'indexer sur l'univers de référence familier au spectateur. D'autre part il manipule cette réalité et joue ainsi un rôle dans l'argumentation. *La verbena de la Paloma* nous présente l'image stéréotypée des bas quartiers madrilènes. C'est l'ambiance plus pittoresque que réaliste de presque toutes les saynètes. C'est l'image du Madrid préindustriel, figée comme un mythe. Image qui correspond bien plus à l'idée qu'on se fait de la ville, qu'à la réalité beaucoup moins agréable. Nous avons affaire à un Madrid traditionnel où s'élimine toute trace de changement et de misère sociale (pensons au flot d'immigrants à la fin du siècle dernier) (Del Moral 1992). Un Madrid qui se caractérise toujours par la sociabilité, le culte de la conversation, et les fêtes populaires (les fameuses scènes 'costumbristas').

J'espère avoir démontré qu'à divers niveaux de son oeuvre, Ricardo de la Vega a eu recours aux clichés et stéréotypes. Cet usage est conforme aux visées essentielles du petit genre, à savoir une consommation massive, rapide et aisée, une identification affective et l'adhésion des esprits au message de la pièce. Les clichés et stéréotypes sont manipulés de telle façon que la réalité est embellie: ce n'est plus la réalité mais la vision que la Restauration aimait tant propager dans les saynètes: un monde animé et de fêtes, peuplé de gens pauvres mais honnêtes, qui tiennent en haute estime des valeurs comme la famille, le travail, l'honneur et la patrie, et, surtout, qui se contentent de ce qu'ils n'ont pas.

Il est évident que si l'usage efficace de clichés et de stéréotypes constitue la force de *La verbena de la Paloma*, c'est en même temps le point faible du petit genre. Les possibilités d'une telle forme dramatique ne sont certainement pas illimitées. La progression de nouvelles modalités comme les variétés et le 'genre infime' n'a donc rien de surprenant.

Notes

1. Précisons que dix des quinze pièces recueillies proviennent des années 1890-1900.

2. Quelques autres premières de 1894: *Boda, tragedia y guateque o el difunto de Chuchita* (saynète, livret de Javier de Burgos, musique de Miguel Marqués, première: Eslava, le 9 janvier 1894); *El traje misterioso* (livret de Juan Lorrente de Urraza et Ricardo Curros, musique de Arturo Saco del Valle, première: Eslava, le 16 janvier 1894); *Los lunes del Imparcial* (paso, livret de Tomás Luceño, première: Lara, le 3 février 1894); *Los dineros del sacristán* (zarzuela, livret de Luis de Larra et Mauricio Gullón, musique de Fernández Caballero, première: Eslava, le 24 mars 1894); *Los puritanos* (paso, livret de

Carlos Arniches et Celso Lucio, musique de Quinito Valverde et Torregrosa, première: Eslava, le 31 mars 1894); *Viento en popa* (livret de Fiacro Irayzoz, musique de Jiménez, première: Eslava, le 5 avril 1894); *El pie izquierdo* (juguete, livret de Carlos Arniches et Celso Lucio, première: Lara, le 12 avril 1894); *¡Al santo, al santo!* (zarzuela, livret de Miguel Echegaray, musique de Quinito Valverde, première: Apolo, le 5 mai 1894); *Las amapolas*, zarzuela, livret de Carlos Arniches y Celso Lucio, musique de Torregrosa, première: Apolo, le 21 juin 1894); *Campanero y sacristán* (zarzuela, livret de Enrique Ayuso et Manuel de Labra, musique de Fernández Caballero et Hermoso, première: Príncipe Alfonso, le 14 août 1894); *La boronda* (juguete, livret de Javier de Burgos, première: Lara, le 3 novembre 1894).

3. Un exemple connu est *¿Cuántas calentitas, cuántas?* de Tomás Luceño (1868).

4. On pourrait les considérer comme la réincarnation des *manolos* y *manolas* des saynètes du XVIIIe siècle.

Bibliographie

Amossy, R. et E. Rosen, *Les discours du cliché*. Paris: CDU/CEDES, 1982.

Deleito y Piñuela, J., *Origen y apogeo del género chico*. Madrid: Revista de Occidente, 1949.

Garrido Gallardo, M.A., 'Notas sobre el sainete como género literario', dans: *El teatro menor en España a partir del siglo XVI*, Madrid: CSIC, 1983.

Moral, C. del, 'La mitificación de Madrid en el género chico', dans: *Revista de Occidente*, nr. 128 (1992).

Valencia, A. (ed.), *El género chico. (Antología de textos completos)* Madrid: Taurus, 1962.

Yxart, J., *El arte escénico en España*. Barcelona: Alta Fulla, 1987.

Egil Törnqvist
IBSEN AND STRINDBERG CONQUER PARIS

1894 was an important year for Scandinavian drama. Not because August Strindberg wrote or published any play in that year; he did not. And certainly not because any remarkable productions originated in Scandinavia, where the theatre of the 1890s on the whole was very traditional, dominated by French drawing-room drama of the Scribean well-made type.

It is true that Bjørnstjerne Bjørnson completed his *Over Ævne (Beyond Human Power)*, Part II in that year. And that Henrik Ibsen published his *Lille Eyolf (Little Eyolf)* toward the end of the year. But if we use the emergence of important new plays as a criterion, practically every year in this period becomes important in Scandinavia thanks to the three playwrights just mentioned.

The reason why 1894 is a remarkable year in the history of Scandinavian theatre is, rather, that it was in that year that plays by Bjørnson, Ibsen and Strindberg were successfully staged in Paris, so much so that we may speak of a Scandinavian breakthrough in what was unquestionably the capital of European theatre. At least four Scandinavian plays were warmly received: Bjørnson's *Over Ævne (Au delà des Forces)*, Ibsen's *Et Dukkehjem (Maison de Poupée)*, and Strindberg's *Fordringsägare (Créanciers)* and *Fadren (Père)*.

Until then all three playwrights, often associated with Antoine's Théâtre Libre, had been generally regarded as naturalist playwrights. Now they were staged at the prime symbolist theatre, Lugné-Poe's Théâtre de l'Oeuvre. Lugné-Poe, merely twenty-five at the time, even took his production of *Bygmester Solness (Solness le Constructeur)*, this too produced in 1894, to Christiania and of *Créanciers* to Stockholm in October of that same year.

As a dramatist Bjørnson, now rarely performed outside his own country, was actually the forerunner of both Ibsen and Strindberg. During the 1890s several of his plays were staged in Paris. In 1893 Antoine performed his social drama *En Fallit (Une Faillite)*. The following year his religious play *Over Ævne*, Part I, was staged at Théâtre de l'Oeuvre, while *En Hanske (Un Gant)* and *Léonarda* were done as private performances. Yet none of these productions attracted nearly as much attention as those based on Ibsen's and Strindberg's dramas. I shall therefore limit myself to the lastmentioned playwrights — also because their plays are now, a hundred years later, still regularly performed all over the world. We are therefore, in their case, in a better position to compare production and reception in 1894 with the situation today.

In the period 1890-97 no less than fourteen Ibsen plays were done in Paris, most of them at the Théâtre de l'Oeuvre. After *Gengangere (Revenants)*, the first Ibsen play to be done in the French capital — at Antoine's Théâtre Libre — followed *Vildanden (Le Canard sauvage)*, *Hedda Gabler* and *Fruen fra havet (La Dame de la mer)*. In 1893 the Théâtre de l'Oeuvre opened with *Rosmersholm*, followed by *En Folkefiende (Un Ennemi du peuple)*. The following year

Bygmester Solness and *Et Dukkehjem* were performed. In 1895 *Lille Eyolf* (*Le Petit Eyolf*), *Brand* and *Samfundets Støtter* (*Les Soutiens de la société*) were done, the following year *Peer Gynt*. The Ibsen cycle at the Théâtre de l'Oeuvre was concluded with *Kjærlighedens Komedie* (*La Comédie de l'amour*) and *John Gabriel Borkman* in 1897, in which year Lugné-Poe ceased to produce both Scandinavian and symbolist theatre.

Measured in plays performed, Strindberg's success was, by comparison, modest. *Fröken Julie* (*Mademoiselle Julie*) was done in 1893, *Fordringsägare* (*Créanciers*) and *Fadren* (*Père*) a year later. Yet the last two plays were more successful than most of Ibsen's dramas.

During the Third Republic Paris was the cultural centre of the world. For a dramatist recognition in Paris meant an international breakthrough — as Strindberg clarifies in his drama *Brott och brott* (*Crimes and Crimes*). No wonder that both Bjørnson and Strindberg settled in Paris for some time. No wonder that Ibsen after the premiere of *Maison de poupée* sent a telegram to Gabrielle Réjane, who did the part of Nora, that read: "My loftiest dream has come true, Réjane has done Nora in Paris."[1]

This does not mean that the Scandinavian playwrights were immediately and generally accepted by the Parisians. The critics were, in fact, very divided. One reason for this is that the Scandinavian plays were staged in a period when naturalism, associated especially with the Théâtre Libre, represented an illusionistic type of theatre, very different from the kind relished by the symbolists of the Théâtre d'Art and the Théâtre de l'Oeuvre. Another reason is that French chauvinists could not easily accept the idea that foreign playwrights would outshine the native ones — Scribe, Sardou, Augier, Dumas *fils*, Becque, Zola, Goncourt — writers who, after all, were internationally well-known. A third reason is that the Scandinavian plays neither formally nor thematically agreed with the French cultural and theatrical tradition. As a result they often seemed unintelligible to the critics who were used to the rational logics of the Scribean *pièce bien faite*.

The years 1892-94 were marked by an intensification of violent anarchism in France. There were eleven bomb explosions in Paris and several assassinations. When Ibsen's *Un Ennemi du peuple*, with its display of the rottenness of (bourgeois) society, opened at the Bouffes du Nord in November 1893, it was introduced by an anarchist lecturer, the poet Laurent Tailhade, a circumstance that no doubt promoted a political interpretation of the play. In the words of the writer Camille Mauclair:

> Anarchism was the intellectual love of the youth in 1894, and we all took this play as well as Stockmann [its protagonist] to be examples of anarchism — which, in fact, they are not.[2]

Not surprisingly, Ibsen was "quite dissatisfied when he heard of the paradoxes launched in the anarchist Laurent Tailhade's introductory lecture. *En Folkefiende* was lucid enough and did not need any introduction."[3]

About a year later, in October 1894, the Jewish officer Alfred Dreyfus was arrested, accused of having delivered secret documents to the military attaché of the German embassy. Antisemitic and anti-German feelings in France were strengthened and made way for a widespread dislike of foreigners generally. Since the king of Sweden and Norway, Oscar II, was pro-German, this dislike was to affect also the Scandinavians. The difference between Germanic and Latin mentality and culture was in conservative quarters strongly emphasized and there was no doubt about which was the superior culture. In *Le Journal* of 8 August, 1893, you could, for example, read that

> The way of seeing, feeling, expressing feelings and passions, all that constitutes the Norwegian soul, is too different from the French soul. Our race is in love with clarity and logic. We have ardent blood, we love all which is sparkling, pretty, and delicate. As heirs to Mediterranean civilizations we have inherited from them the love of pure and gracious artistic forms. For us, elegance and spirit are qualities which take precedence over others. Uncouthness and vulgarity strangely repel us.[4]

In *La Cocarde*, Charles Maurras similarly declared that "ces barbares nous gâtent l'âme" ('these barbarians', i.e. the Scandinavians, 'destroy our soul'). Praising the Mediterranean culture, he assured the reader that the French had nothing to learn from the Anglo-Germanic or Scandinavian literatures.[5] Henry Fouquier, similarly, after the opening of *Solness le Constructeur*, warned his readers of the new invasion of barbarians from the North.[6] At the same time — and rather inconsistently — the conservative critics considered the Scandinavian playwrights merely offshoots of their French counterparts. Fouquier, who thought Strindberg to be Norwegian, asserted that *Créanciers* owed a debt to Dumas *fils's Une Visite de Noce*. Jules Lemaître held the opinion that the three Scandinavian playwrights were all influenced by Dumas *fils* and Augier. *Père*, he remarked, had great affinities with Edmond de Goncourt's *Charles Demailly*.[7] In an article entitled 'De l'influence récente des littératures du Nord', where Strindberg is thought to be a Dane, Lemaître claims that Ibsen's Nora is but a Norwegian counterpart of George Sand's Lélia, his Hedda Gabler merely a Norwegian equivalent of her Indiana, and that, in fact, most of Ibsen's ideas could be found in the work of this French writer.[8] Georg Brandes, the leading Scandinavian critic at the time, countered this by pointing out, in the international journal *Cosmopolis* (January 1897), that Ibsen had assured him that he had never read a single book by George Sand — while refraining from mentioning that his wife was deeply impressed by this writer — and that all he had learned from Dumas *fils* was how to avoid the mistakes he frequently discovered in the dramas of this French playwright. Whatever is true concerning such particulars, there is no doubt about the fact that there is a shrill contrast between the chauvinistic French outbursts and the stagnation of French drama and theatre at the time. Already in 1881 Zola had declared that the naturalist theatre was 'la nouvelle formule', the new form of drama that should replace the artificial Scribean play of intrigue. Yet many questioned the suitability of plotless, deterministic naturalism for the dramatic genre, and as late as 1887 Jacques Saint-Cère could still complain, in *Revue d'Art Dramatique*: "The time has come, when we in France have to find a new dramatic form. It is high time!"[9] In the same year Strindberg, who had just completed *Fadren*, proudly declared: "The young Frenchmen still seek the formula; I have found it!" Evidently regarding himself as a naturalist at the time, Strindberg had indeed discovered a viable dramatic form — but it was hardly a naturalist one.

What then are the typical traits of the plays both the French naturalists and symbolists disliked? Characteristic of the Scribean well-made play is that the recipient is continually kept informed as the complicated plot enfolds. Little is left unsaid or unclear. The audience is usually better informed than any single character, and much of the enjoyment consists in observing how the 'ignorant' characters behave in circumstances familiar to the spectator. It is, incidentally, interesting to see that this type of drama has much in common with present-day television soap opera — the well-made play of our time.

The grand old man among the French critics, Francisque Sarcey, was born and bred with the Scribean *pièce bien faite*. This explains Sarcey's negative view of Ibsen, whose plays in many respects are constructed quite differently. Ibsen actually strove to rid himself of the drawing-room monosetting — still adhered to in *Et Dukkehjem* and *Gengangere* — that was so closely connected with the *pièce bien faite* and, for other reasons, with naturalist drama. In his attempts to break out of the French salon, Ibsen more and more included exterior scenes in his plays and, as Brandell notes, ingeniously exploited the Scandinavian glass veranda, "which is interior and exterior at the same time."[10]

Since the structure of the well-made play was identified as French, "the introduction of a different dramatic structure", Deak points out, "was perceived as a threat not only to established theater but also to contemporary French society's entire value system."[11] It was especially Ibsen's retrospective presentation of the past — his technique of gradual revelation — that bothered the French critics. It is characteristic that when the naturalist writer Henry Céard read *Revenants* to Antoine, he offered to add a prologue that would explain the prescenic events.[12] "I don't go to theater to figure out enigmas", Sarcey declared. "It's up to the author to explain himself and to say clearly what he wants me to know."[13] Rather than mystification, or 'Nordic mist' as they called it, most French critics wanted clarification.

In England Ibsen had an influential supporter in William Archer who, well versed in Norwegian, not only translated the plays but also directed some of them. In France, by contrast, the plays were translated by a Lithuanian count, Moritz Prozor, who knew more Swedish than Norwegian and had little experience of the theatre. And the plays were directed either by Lugné-Poe or, in most cases, by the Danish writer and theatre man Herman Bang.

Unlike Archer, Lugné-Poe applied to Ibsen's plays the solemn, monotonous acting style he had used for Maeterlinck's pieces. Similarly, Maeterlinck's 'A Propos de Solness le Constructeur', published in *Le Figaro*, on 12 April, 1894, that is, the day before the play opened, seems to imply a symbolist acting style like the one practiced at the l'Oeuvre:

> There is sorcery in them [Solness and Hilde], as in all of us. I believe that Hilde and Solness are the first dramatic heroes who feel for an instant that they are living in the atmosphere of the soul. And this essential life which they discover behind the every day life strikes them with terror....
> Their conversation resembles nothing that we have ever heard, since Ibsen had attempted to blend in the same utterance both the interior and exterior dialogue. A new inexpressible power dominates this somnambulistic drama.[14]

The dialogue between Hilde and Solness came close to Lugné-Poe's dream

> of a theater in which there is no acting but where two actors interpret everything that their souls possess by means of the modulated sound of their voices, like a never-ending song....

In a revealing, seemingly anti-theatrical statement, which points forward to the theatre of the ear, radio drama, Lugné-Poe declared:

> Everything that is of the flesh is repulsive.... Beauty lives only in voices which are not of the flesh.[15]

Prozor, who evidently feared that Lugné-Poe would turn *Rosmersholm* into a symbolist experiment, asked Herman Bang, who was quite opposed to the symbolist style of acting,[16] to be present during the rehearsals.[17] Bang has given us a very vivid but surprisingly little known description of the l'Oeuvre acting style as practiced in *Rosmersholm*. In an article in a Norwegian newspaper he relates:

> They were already rehearsing when I arrived. They began with the second act, and I saw immediately that I had fallen right into the midst of a symbolist theater. They acted Ibsen as if they were doing *Pelléas and Mélisande*. The mise-en-scène of *Rosmersholm* is without any firm contours. The actors wander restlessly over the stage, resembling shadows drifting continuously on the wall. They like to move with their arms spread out, their elbows at their sides, and fingers stretched out like the apostles in old paintings who look as if they had been surprised during worship.
> The diction corresponds to this strange appearance. The contours of the lines are erased in an ascending and descending chant that is

never-ending in its monotony. Like in a Russian hymn, its aim is to create a single ongoing mood, and it takes the life out of the individual words by weaving them into some kind of spoken song.
It was obvious that the intention was to create a gloomy atmosphere. All colors, all details, were erased in order to achieve it. 'The white horses' were the main character in this production of *Rosmersholm*. Rosmer's estate was enveloped in a bizarre and ghostlike atmosphere in which the characters appeared like shadows, strange sleepwalkers mumbling barely recognizable words, the victim of a secret nightmare.[18]

Familiar as he was with the original Norwegian text, Bang translated anew passages that appeared obscure in Prozor's version. Firmness in blocking, he insisted, would lead to firmness in dialogue. His comments on the opening of the play gives a rather good idea of his sensitive and surprisingly modern directorial approach:

The stage should be half lighted. The two women talk in low voices as one naturally does at dusk. Kroll enters the room carefully with hesitation in his speech and eyes, as if he were walking through a swamp or a morass. Rebecca's answers should be vague: questioning with her eyes, always covering her face like somebody who tells many lies. She appears on guard, as if she senses danger. Their voices should be disinterested, but Kroll's voice should have an underlying layer of insight, and Rebecca's voice should reflect a calculated caution which indicates her guilt. The tone of voice, their glances, should in every instant reflect the steel dagger that they both hide under their coats, ready to use in a battle. With its subdued atmosphere, pauses full of meaning, secrets confessed through a body position or a glance, this scene will be like the overture of the play, a mute overture in which all the themes of the play, dimly lighted, glide in and out....[19]

Ibsen saw this production when the Théâtre de l'Oeuvre brought it to Christiania. However, he seems to have been less impressed by it than by l'Oeuvre's *Solness le Constructeur*. Already before this play was produced in Paris, Ibsen urged French artists intending to stage the play not to look for symbols in it but rather pay attention to the aspects of real life. "Otherwise they would make my work incomprehensible", he warned.[20] Although he told Bang that the l'Oeuvre production meant "the resurrection of his play",[21] he indicated to Lugné-Poe that he was not altogether satisfied with the style of acting, assuring him that he wished his work to "be played passionately and not otherwise". His remark had an immediate effect on Lugné-Poe:

Ibsen, in one second, by one word, had changed the entire nature of my languid and somewhat psalmodizing interpretation of Solness.

Nevertheless it was only after two years that the character became totally modified.[22]

Seen as an authority with regard to his own plays, Ibsen was someone Lugné-Poe could respect. It was presumably more difficult to accept a rival director like Bang as a 'teacher'. Yet it is likely that Bang's psychologically sensitive approach to the plays meant more to Lugné-Poe than Ibsen's statements. Georg Brandes' brother Edvard disapproved of the symbolist style of acting in Lugné-Poe's Christiania guest performances. If this is the way Ibsen is performed in France, he remarked, the irritation of the French critics is understandable.[23] One of the irritated critics was, of course, Sarcey, who in his review of *Solness le Constructeur*, had earlier protested against what he considered a way of acting Ibsen that stemmed from Germany. "In the German theatre", he wrote,

> it has become a tradition (...) when they play Ibsen, that they strive to make the audience forget that these are real people of flesh and blood whom they see treading the boards. They move but little, use almost no hand gestures and, when they do, make them broad, almost sacerdotal. Their whole recitation is characterized by a slow recitation, which seems to emanate from supernatural and symbolic lips.[24]

Much more successful with the Parisians than *Solness le Constructeur* was *Maison de poupée*, which opened on 20 April 1894 at Théâtre Vaudeville. The manager, Paul Porel, had called in Herman Bang to direct it. Gabrielle Réjane as Nora, Bang writes in his memoirs,

> revolted against her husband, her fate, against love, and against herself. (...) Nora left Helmer and all his household, and she left unbroken and as the greater of the two. In this leave-taking scene, she went as someone who has finally thrown off her own shackles and freed herself.[25]

Far from seeing Réjane's Nora as a victorious *révolteuse*, Sarcey found her altogether too afraid, "terrorized out of all proportion to the reality of the situation":

> And we all say to ourselves, in Paris at any rate: Why is Nora so upset about so small a thing [the altruistic forgery]? She has only to explain the matter to her husband.... She cries, she throws herself in his arms, but she does not say to him the one thing she should say, which we are all waiting to hear: 'I was wrong, but it was for you that I compromised myself....' (...) Helmer would be the last person to bear a grudge for her imprudence, since it was to save his life that this imprudent act was committed.[26]

Ever since *Et Dukkehjem* was first published, it has been discussed to what extent Nora should be regarded as a representative of her gender. Having seen Mrs. Alving, Hedda Gabler and Nora, Edmond de Goncourt was ready to conclude, in his *Journal*, that "a naive nature, a sophistic temperament, and a perverse heart are characteristic of Scandinavian women."[27] Despite such misgivings, the play as a whole was enthusiastically received. Louis Ganderax, in *Revue Hebdomadaire*, for example, declared that "après le roman russe, est arrivé le drame scandinave" (after the Russian novel, the Scandinavian drama has come).[28] For the first time Ibsen was victorious on the Parisian stage.

More eager to conquer Paris than either Bjørnson or Ibsen, Strindberg felt that a recognition there would serve as a lesson for his countrymen who were too traditional and too provincial to understand his true significance.[29] Unlike the other Scandinavian playwrights, Strindberg actually wrote his so-called naturalistic plays with an eye to the Paris stage. But he had to wait several years before his dreams were fulfilled. Moreover, his success, unlike Ibsen's, was to be short-lived. Not until after the first world war was he performed in Paris again and not until after the second one did he become a serious rival of the great Norwegian playwright.

The first Strindberg play to be done in Paris is also the play for which he is internationally best known: *Fröken Julie*. Yet the 1893 Paris premiere of *Mademoiselle Julie* at the Théâtre Libre, on a triple bill together with a now forgotten curtain-raiser and a new play by Edmond de Goncourt, was hardly a success. On the morning of the premiere Goncourt, who like Lemaître thought that Strindberg was a Dane, published a violent attack on the foreign dramatists in *L'Écho de Paris*, concluding that "if we need a guiding star for our modern theatre, it is neither to Tolstoy nor to Ibsen that French thought should turn, but to ... Beaumarchais."[30] Ironically, Antoine noted in his diary, Goncourt, "this great champion of life and truth, this revolutionary, talks of Swedes and Norwegians with the same lack of understanding, the same prejudice as do his hated rivals Sarcey and Pessard."[31] Another irony was that Strindberg in his preface to *Fröken Julie* had declared that he had learned more from the novels of the Goncourt brothers than from any other writers. Of great interest — in view of the weight Artaud was later to attach to the word 'cruelty' — is a statement in *Revue des Deux Mondes* of 1 November 1893:

> M. Strindberg is not a true realist; rather his harsh and acrid elo-
> quence, his indictments against society, the taste which leads him to
> depict the ugliness of life and the soul without restraint (...) without
> shame, epitomize the literature of cruelty.[32]

Much more successful than *Mademoiselle Julie* was *Créanciers*, which opened at the Comédie parisienne on 21 June 1894 as a Théâtre de l'Oeuvre production with Lugné-Poe as director as well as in the role of Adolf. The play had been translated into French by Strindberg himself and revised for the production by the young dramatist Georges Loiseau.[33] When revising the play Loiseau, who knew no Swedish and little German, nevertheless compared Strindberg's French translation with Erich Holm's German one, which had just appeared. As a result he changed Strindberg's translation by adding lines and stage directions which the author himself had omitted when turning his text into French. Since he also retained the additional phrases Strindberg had put into his French translation, Loiseau's version of *Fordringsägare* became much more circumstantial than the two Strindbergian versions. An interesting case in point, brought forward by Engwall, are the crutches in the opening stage directions: "*Adolf and Gustav are at the table, right. Adolf is sculpting a wax figure on a small stand. Propped up near him are his crutches.*" Here, in the original version, Strindberg indicates Adolf's poor health by placing two crutches next to him. But in the French translation he omits them. Loiseau, who discovered the crutches in Holm's German translation, reintroduced them in his revised version. When rehearsing the play, the actors wished to tone down Adolf's epilepsy by omitting the crutches. Loiseau disagreed. To solve the conflict the actors and the director, on the one hand, Loiseau, on the other, turned to Strindberg. His reply was laconic: "Rayez les béquilles s.v.p!" (Delete the crutches, please!).

The premiere of *Créanciers* opened with an introductory lecture by Lucien Muhlfeld, the editor of *Revue Blanche*, who took the opportunity of attacking Sarcey and other critics present in the audience. While Bang's one-acter *Frères*, which preceded Strindberg's play was coolly received, the critics were enthusiastic about *Créanciers*. Even Henri Fouquier, this confirmed opponent of Scandinavian writing, was fairly positive. And Sarcey was less hostile to it than he had been to any of Ibsen's plays. Henry Bauer, a staunch supporter of Strindberg, saw it as the antithesis of Ibsen's *Maison de poupée*.[34] "Where do you find such a violent pleading against the liberation of woman?", he asked — a rhetorical question that makes one wonder whether the positive reaction to *Créanciers* among the male critics might not have something to do with a secretely nourished sympathy for Strindberg's misogynist leanings.

"Grande triomphe", Lugné-Poe cabled to Strindberg after the premiere. The playwright was rapturous. "This is happiness", he wrote to a friend, "this sense of power, sitting in a hut on the Danube among six women who regard me as a semi-idiot, and knowing that in Paris, the intellectual centre of the world, 500 people are sitting in an auditorium silent as mice, stupid enough to expose their brains to my powers of suggestion."[35]

After the success of *Créanciers* Lugné-Poe was willing to stage also *Fadren*, which had been published in a French translation by Strindberg himself already in 1888. The premiere of *Père* took place on 13 December 1894 at the Nouveau Théâtre, one of the largest theatres in Paris, holding over a thousand spectators. Many prominent Parisians had come to the opening, Rodin and Gauguin being among them. Bang had directed the play in his usual psychological manner. Lugné-Poe took the small part of the Pastor.

Strindberg's ending, apparently considered too strenuous for the audience, was changed. Instead of having the Captain suffer a stroke on the stage, leaving him unconscious, Bang's Captain was, mentally broken, helped off the stage at the end. This and some other changes were made with Strindberg's approval. By omitting longish passages, he reasoned, the director merely made the play more attractive to the audience. "Perhaps I can break Ibsen's record", he said, adding that the Norwegian playwright was "too heavy for the Parisians."[36]

Père was warmly received by the critics and had a comparatively long run. Sarcey found Strindberg theatrically superior not only to Bjørnson but also to Ibsen. Bauer considered the production "the first indisputable victory of the Scandinavian literature in Paris."[37] And, echoing this view, Camille Mauclair stated:

> Last night we witnessed the Scandinavian theatre's first great and unquestioned success in Paris. We have had excellent evenings before, Antoine's *Ghosts*, *A Doll's House* at the Vaudeville, but these were successes for the actors or for tragic effects. Strindberg has achieved his triumph through his ideas, through the irreconcilable violence of his piercing and brutally realistic genius.[38]

While the two Norwegians and the Swede provided Antoine and Lugné-Poe with texts of a kind and quality lacking in contemporary French drama, it was the Dane Herman Bang rather than the two French directors who most of all contributed to the successful staging of the Scandinavian plays. With his commitment and energy (rehearsals could last from early morning until late evening), psychological sensitivity and outstanding directorial talent — not the least his ability to adjust the 'Scandinavian' roles to the French actors — Bang was, in Lugné-Poe's opinion, nothing less than the major director in the 1890s.[39] Nevertheless,

> (...) it was Lugné-Poe who took credit for all the productions. Bang's name was not even mentioned in the French press in connection with l'Oeuvre. Only the Norwegian newspapers mentioned Bang's involvement (...) Later, in his memoirs, Lugné-Poe gave Bang due credit for the direction of the Scandinavian plays. It took him thirty-seven years to do it (...)[40]

As we have seen, the Scandinavians literally and figuratively entered the Parisian stage at a time when the well-made play had become *vieux jeu* and naturalism had lost much of its impetus and was giving way to symbolism. Although the reception of the Bjørnson, Ibsen and Strindberg productions for various reasons was not favourable with all the critics, there is little doubt that 1894 was an important year of recognition for the three playwrights. While Bjørnson and Ibsen were to pen only a few more plays after this date,

Strindberg was still to publish his historical dramas as well as his pioneering dream and chamber plays. The Parisian successes of 1894 may well have contributed to his return to playwriting in January, 1898 when, still in Paris, he began to write the first part of his trilogy *Till Damaskus* (*To Damascus*), the play that was to change the course of modern drama.

IBSEN AND STRINDBERG ON THE PARIS STAGE

Playwright	Play	Paris premiere
Ibsen	*Gengangere* *Revenants* *Ghosts*	30 May 1890, Théâtre Libre
Ibsen	*Vildanden* *Le Canard sauvage* *The Wild Duck*	28 April 1891, Théâtre Libre
Ibsen	*Hedda Gabler*	17 December 1891, Théâtre du Vaudeville
Ibsen	*Fruen fra havet* *La Dame de la mer* *The Lady from the Sea*	16 December 1892, Théâtre Moderne (Cercle des Escholiers)
Strindberg	*Fröken Julie* *Mademoiselle Julie* *Miss Julie*	16 January 1893, Théâtre Libre
Ibsen	*Rosmersholm*	6 October 1893, Théâtre de l'Oeuvre
Ibsen	*En Folkefiende* *Un Ennemi du peuple* *An Enemy of the People*	10 November 1893, Théâtre de l'Oeuvre
Ibsen	*Bygmester Solness* *Solness le Constructeur* *The Masterbuilder*	3 April 1894, Théâtre de l'Oeuvre
Ibsen	*Et Dukkehjem* *Maison de poupée* *A Doll's House*	20 April 1894, Théâtre du Vaudeville

Strindberg	*Fordringsägare* *Créanciers* *Creditors*	21 June 1894, Théâtre de l'Oeuvre
Strindberg	*Fadren* *Père* *The Father*	13 December 1894, Théâtre de l'Oeuvre
Ibsen	*Lille Eyolf* *Le Petit Eyolf* *Little Eyolf*	8 May 1895, Théâtre de l'Oeuvre
Ibsen	*Brand*	22 June 1895, Théâtre de l'Oeuvre
Ibsen	*Samfundets Støtter* *Les Soutiens de la* *société* *Pillars of Society*	23 June 1896, Théâtre de l'Oeuvre
Ibsen	*Peer Gynt*	12 November 1896, Théâtre de l'Oeuvre
Ibsen	*Kjærlighedens Komedie* *La Comédie de l'amour* *Love's Comedy*	23 June 1897, Théâtre de l'Oeuvre
Ibsen	*John Gabriel Borkman*	9 November 1897, Théâtre de l'Oeuvre

Notes

1. Gerhard Gran, *Henrik Ibsen: Liv og verker*, II (Christiania, 1918), p. 82.

2. Camille Mauclair, *Servitude et Grandeur Littéraire* (Paris, 1922), p. 108. Quoted from Gunnar Ahlström, *Strindbergs erövring av Paris: Strindberg och Frankrike* (Stockholm, 1956) p. 108.

3. A. Lugné-Poe, *Ibsen i Frankrike*, trans. Sigurd Høst (Oslo, 1938), p. 55.

4. Quoted from Frantisek Deak, *Symbolist Theater: The Formation of an Avant-Garde* (Baltimore and London, 1993) p. 193.

5. 29 November, 1894. Quoted from Ahlström, p. 235.

6. Ahlström, p. 244.

7. Ahlström, p. 237.

8. *Revue des Deux Mondes*, 15 December, 1894, p. 238.

9. Quoted from Kela Nyholm, "Henrik Ibsen paa den franske Scene", *Ibsen-Årbok 1957-59*, ed. Einar Østvedt (Oslo, 1959), p. 11.

10. Gunnar Brandell, *Nordiskt drama – studier och belysningar* (Uppsala, 1993), p. 47.

11. Deak, p. 198.

12. Nyholm, p. 29.

13. Francisque Sarcey, *Quarante ans de théâtre*, Vol. 13 (Paris, 1902), p. 349.

14. Quoted from Deak, p. 204.

15. Lugné-Poe in *Bergens Tidende*, 28 July, 1894. Quoted from Deak, p. 216.

16. Hanne Amsinck, *Sceneinstruktøren Herman Bang og det franske symbolistiske teater* (København, 1972), pp. 53, 65, 71, 82.

17. Mette Borg, *Sceneinstruktøren Herman Bang* (Copenhagen), 1986, p. 17.

18. "Blade i min dagbok", *Bergens Tidende*, 18 October, 1893. Quoted from Deak, p. 189.

19. "Blade i min dagbok". Quoted from Deak, p. 190.

20. Interview by L. François in *Revue d'Art Dramatique*, Jan. 1894, p. 14.

21. Nyholm, p. 49.

22. Aurélien Lugné-Poe, *Acrobaties* (Paris, 1931), pp. 111-12.

23. Nyholm, p. 49.

24. Quoted from Meyer, *Ibsen*, p. 734.

25. Herman Bang, *Masker og Mennesker* (Copenhagen, 1910), pp. 176-7.

26. *Quarante ans de théâtre*, Vol. 8 (Paris, 1902), pp. 359, 361. Quoted from Frederick J. and Lise-Lone Marker, *Ibsen's Lively Art: A Performance Study of the Major Plays* (Cambridge, 1989), pp. 61-2.

27. Quoted from Nyholm, p. 59.

28. Quoted from Ahlström, p. 232.

29. Cf. Gunnar Brandell, *Strindberg – ett författarliv*, III (Stockholm, 1983), p. 15.

30. Edmond de Goncourt in *L'Écho de Paris*. Quoted from Michael Meyer, *Strindberg: A Biography* (Oxford and New York, 1987), p. 261.

31. Ahlström, pp. 158-9.

32. Quoted from Christopher Innes, *Avant Garde Theatre 1892-1992* (London and New York, 1993), p. 239, note 32.

33. For a comparison between Strindberg's and Loiseau's version, see Gunnel Engwall, "Frenchifying *Fordringsägare*", *Strindberg and Genre*, ed. Michael Robinson (Norwich, 1991), pp. 137-47.

34. Bauer in *L'Écho de Paris*. Quoted from Ahlström, p. 213.

35. August Strindberg, *Brev,* Vol. X (Stockholm, 1981ff), p. 130. Quoted from Meyer, *Strindberg*, pp. 296-7.

36. Quoted from Ahlström, p. 249.

37. Bauer in *L'Écho de Paris*. Quoted from Ahlström, p. 253.

38. Mauclair in *Revue Encyclopédique*. Quoted from Meyer, *Strindberg*, p. 311.

39. Amsinck, p. 59.

40. Deak, p. 214.

Henk van der Liet
ON IBSEN IN ANARCHIST RÉGIE,
THE COPENHAGEN STAGE IN THE 1890s·
AND HOLGER DRACHMANN'S SHOT AT WORLD FAME

As Mr. Törnqvist points out in the introduction to his paper 'Ibsen and Strindberg conquer Paris', the 1890s was a remarkable era in Scandinavian theatre-history, and in Scandinavian literary history as a whole. The influence of the two major Scandinavian playwrights in this period, Henrik Ibsen (1828-1906) and August Strindberg (1849-1912), was felt all over Europe. As Törnqvist demonstrates, they had a short-lived but major impact on the Parisian *avant-garde* around Lugné-Poe (1869-1940) and his *Theatre de l'Oeuvre*. We also know that Ibsen, and Strindberg as well, had similar, but longer lasting influence in the German-speaking countries. In more general terms, Scandinavians, and in particular, Norwegian authors, became vastly popular in symbolist circles in Germany and Austria in the 1890s. Among the most important of them are: Knut Hamsun (1859-1952), Jonas Lie (1833-1908), Alexander Kielland (1849-1906) and, last but not least, Arne Garborg (1851-1924), whose novel *Weary Men*[1] became one of the model texts of the German decadent fin de siècle literature.[2]

In this response to Törnqvist's paper, I would like to highlight certain elements that could be of some interest. I would like to emphasize the particular role of the Danish author-director Herman Bang (1857-1912), and the importance of the radical political context in which the Scandinavian plays were staged and received in Paris in the mid-1890s. As we are dealing with Scandinavian theater, I would, furthermore, like to take a closer look at the particular situation in Danish theatre around the year 1894, and pay some attention to the case of the, now largely forgotten, Danish author-playwright, Holger Drachmann (1846-1908).

Success in exile

In his introduction, Mr. Törnqvist briefly touches upon the fact that the productions staged in Scandinavia itself in this era were, on the whole, of a rather traditional nature. Thus, we are confronted with the interesting phenomenon that, generally speaking, the most important Scandinavian playwrights of the era were, for once in Scandinavian theatre history, very influential abroad. They made their breakthrough abroad and, thus, overcame the greatest opponent of Scandinavian authors in their quest for recognition, the language barrier. We know, of course, that playwrights, and this goes as well for other writers and artists, especially in the 19th century, often lived outside Scandinavia for longer periods, often grouping together in the major cultural centers on the continent such as Berlin, Rome, and Paris, albeit they seldom stayed abroad in exile for a lifetime, or adopted a foreign language entirely.[3] Thus Scandinavian artists abroad, kept in close contact with each other, with their cultural background and with their native tongues.

In the mid-1890s, Ibsen had just returned to Norway after nearly 30 years of living abroad in various cities on the continent, while Strindberg was, so to speak, on his way to Paris, arriving there in the fall of 1894. As a matter of fact, Strindberg rented the very same flat that the director of his plays in Paris, Herman Bang, just had abandoned.[4] What we see in this period is more than just coincidental. One may regard the last decade of the 19th century as an era of internationalization of Scandinavian art, theatre, and literature. Furthermore, it is very significant that Norway, whose political, economic and artistic traditions were furthest away from the European cultural mainstream, gained a strong artistic momentum during the last decades of the 19th century, not least in the center of European high-culture, Paris.

Törnqvist gives two main explanations for the fact that Scandinavian drama was so successful in Paris in the early 1890s. The first is that these plays suited the artistic intentions of the *avant-garde* theatre, notably the one represented by Lugné-Poe. The other is that these plays fitted well into the social and political climate of the period. With respect to the way Scandinavian drama was initially perceived, and the transformations these plays were subject to, Törnqvist also draws attention to the importance of Herman Bang as a mediator and his efforts in respect to the *mise-en-scène* of most of the Scandinavian plays performed during the season 1893-94. In this season, eleven Scandinavian plays were staged in Paris, of which ten were staged with the help of, or directed under the auspices of, Bang. Furthermore, it is interesting to note that Bang did not receive any payment at all for his work in Paris as mediator and director, nor did he gain any other financial benefits from these productions. Bang had to earn a living by writing for Scandinavian journals, papers, weeklies, etc.[5] Nevertheless, Bang was not worse off than other Scandinavian authors who had to live solely by their pen and who were heavily dependent on their publishers. Thus, it was actually fame and honour Bang and the other Scandinavians earned in Paris and, as so often is the case with immaterial values of this kind, both the fame and the honour vanished quickly after 1897.

Although the plays by Bjørnson (1832-1910), Strindberg, and, especially, Ibsen, suited the symbolist intentions of Lugné-Poe, it also clear that Herman Bang, who, by the way, despised symbolist drama[6], tried to save the Scandinavian plays involved from being utterly misinterpreted as staged by Lugné-Poe. Thus, the question may be asked whether or not Ibsen and the other Scandinavians were merely being exploited as a vehicle for a theatrical programme that they did not sympathize with. In other words, did the French *avant-garde* not simply use Ibsen, for example, as a convenient motive for an entirely different cause than he had intended? Putting the question more generally, was the choice of foreign plays not in itself a gesture of revolt against French bourgeois culture, which was at this time, drenched in an atmosphere of anti-semitism, xenophobia, and stifling nationalism?

At the same time, one may question whether we today have a proper understanding of the cultural and political turmoil in France and especially in Paris
in the 1890's. Does our contemporary stance, our hindsight, not intervene and
blur the image of the interrelationship between the staging of the Scandinavians, and especially Ibsen, and anarchism as a political movement?
Anarchism as an influential intellectual and political movement was at that
time quite different from what the word implies today. It is no surprise that
of all Ibsen's plays, *An Enemy of the People* (1882), fitted best into the social
and political climate of the era.

As Törnqvist mentions, Ibsen did not approve of the introduction to *An
Enemy of the People* by the anarchist poet Laurent Tailhade. Nonetheless, the
staging of Ibsen in Paris was closely linked to the anarchist turmoil that
culminated in the mid-1890s. These links were partly coincidental, which, in
an ironical manner, is shown by the fact that on on April 4, 1894, a day after
the premiere of *Solness le Constructeur* (1892), Tailhade himself got wounded
in a bombing of a restaurant in Paris[7]. Apart from the coincidental, I would
like to argue that, especially, *An Enemy of the People*, fitted seamlessly into the
anarchistic political hype that went all over the continent, not only in its
terrorist manifestations, but also the more philosophical offspring of the
movement. A token of the latter for example was the renewed interest in
Max Stirner's manifesto, *Der Einzige und sein Eigentum* (1843), which was
widely read in the 1890s, not only by political activists, but also by numerous
artists and writers. Stirner's egotistic anarchism appealed to many *fin de siècle*
artists,[8] and also had a notable impact on Scandinavian authors.[9] Stirner's
philosophy focussed on the 'value' of the individual as the basis for social
relationships and, according to Stirner's line of reasoning, one of the
elementary values of human life was to enjoy life and not to let it be
suppressed and controlled by other forces.

One of the main reasons why *An Enemy of the People* fitted so easily into the
context of radical political philosophy must have been the utopian perspectives that are latent in the play, above all in its last two acts. It is obvious in
Ibsen's text that the play's central character, Doctor Stockmann, will not flee
to America. On the contrary, he will stay and, together with his family, the
ones closest and dearest to him, he will try to develop a new humanity. By
means of educating new generations he wants to raise the individual's
morale, and in doing so, to overcome the powers of evil that stimulate the
merging of individual values to the vague concept of a common cause, that
of the 'broad majority'. The utopian and metaphorical references to early
Christian society are quite obvious, for example his call for at least twelve
boys/disciples at the end of the play, and in Doctor Stockmann's speech in
Captain Horster's home, during the grand meeting in the fourth act of the
play.

Another reason for the appeal of *An Enemy of the People* to radical political
Zeitgeist is the fact that this play is one of the very few plays by Ibsen that
deal with the present. In most of his plays, Ibsen ties the cause of events on
stage to the past, mostly in the form of some kind of guilt that has to be

expiated, or the recall of errors committed in the past. Examples of this are, of course, Nora Helmer's forgery in *A Doll's House* and Captain Alving's juvenile sins in *Ghosts*. *An Enemy of the People* is Ibsen's only play which is clearly played against a current and realistic social background.

But it would not do justice to look upon *An Enemy of the People* as a play advocating radical politics. It is, in some sense, a farce or comedy about democratic institutions, but it also makes a butt of the idealistic world-reformer, Dr. Stockmann. Just as in *A Doll's House*, *An Enemy of the People* is imbued with the awakening of a consciousness, a process that leads to external social decay but, at the same time, leads to an increase in individual consciousness and strength. In *An Enemy of the People*, Ibsen demonstrates that the further the individual consciousness develops, the less belief he has in collective solutions.

Ibsen was not a declared anarchist, but neither was he unsympathetic to it, as may be deduced from a letter to Lugné-Poe in which he is supposed to have said, "I am an anarchist and individualist".[10] As early as 1866, Ibsen's letters reveal that he had learned about the most important political *avant-garde* currents and radical philosophy in Europe. Ibsen's plays turned in the 1870s against the state, the church, and bourgeois society in general. In the context of the mid-1890s it can be hardly suprising that Ibsen was easily mentioned in connection with anarchism.[11]

Nevertheless, *An Enemy of the People*, written in 1882, was also to become Ibsen's last explicit social-critical play. Now he turned to introspection, to the psychology of the characters, their spiritual conflicts and their consciousness. In that respect, plays such as *The Wild Duck*, *The Master Builder*, and *When We Dead Awaken* were more in accord with Lugné-Poe's symbolist artistic credo.

The Danish situation

In the last decades of the 19th century, a clear expansion and polarisation of the Danish theatre audience took place. On the one hand, there still existed a very strong traditional mainstream theatre, often nursing the official upper-class and traditional theatrical heritage (e.g. opera, Bournonville's ballets, Holberg, Oehlenschläger, Heiberg). On the other hand, more popular theatrical forms made their way to new groups of spectators in the new settings of the rapidly increasing amount of newly founded stages. But cabaret-types of entertainment also gained influence in high-cultural contexts. One may speak of a rapid emancipation of theatrical forms that formerly were looked upon as strictly lower-class entertainment.

The nineteenth century showed a tremendous activity in Danish theatrical life. Just as in the rest of Europe, many private theatres sprang up. The Royal Theatre in Copenhagen was the dominant stage throughout most of the 19th century, but it lost most of its monopoly after a new theatre bill had passed parliament in 1889. In the following decades, a number of new theatres developed and competed increasingly with the Royal Theatre. Although the new theatre bill opened possibilities for new initiatives, not all restrictions were lifted. One still needed a formal royal privilege to establish a theatre in Denmark, and the new theatres had to limit their activities largely to popular comedy, farce, vaudeville, and the burlesque *Singspiel*, while the Royal Theatre mainly staged classical pieces, ballet, and opera. Furthermore, all these theatres were submitted to the restriction that none of these plays should have been staged at the Royal Theatre in the preceding ten years. The aim of these measures was to secure a strict division between popular and high culture. This implied, for example, that the comic repertory of the Danish 18th century playwright, Ludvig Holberg, was strictly limited to the Royal Theatre and was not to be staged (in the original shape) in popular theatres throughout the 19th century. The most important new stages in Copenhagen were Casino, founded in 1848, and Folketeatret (1857), while the very important Dagmarteater opened in 1883.[12]

The audience for these new theatres may be best described as primarily a middleclass family-audience; the spectators came to be entertained and had no inclinations towards the problem-confrontation-type of plays that the more progressive alternative playwrights aimed at. Thus, it is hardly surprising that progressive playwrights quite often made their breakthrough abroad.[13] These home audiences wanted to be pleased, not shocked. This does not imply that the dramatic experience was not aiming at thrills; as we all know, the shocking and horrifying is often part of entertainment, as is demonstrated by the former popularity of public execution or, to take a more contemporary example, by thrillers and horror movies. But in respect to the middle-class family audiences and the plays staged at popular Copenhagen theatres in the late 1800s, it is obvious that the most popular genres were *folkekomedier* (popular comedy), comic opera, vaudeville, revue, and farce.

The Dagmar Theatre came closest to the repertory of the Royal Theatre. Located just off Town Hall Square and opposite the Tivoli Gardens, it was, in many ways, closely related to the Royal Theatre, as it was built by the very same architect who had been responsible for the new building of the Royal Theatre, which was completed in 1874. Shortly after its opening, it turned out that the Dagmar Theatre's managing-directors and actors were able to compete with, and even outrival, the Royal Theatre's position as the country's leading stage. As a matter of fact, leading actors that had broken away from the Royal Theatre helped the new stage to become a more attractive arena for new theatrical developments than the Royal Theatre, which, in return became more and more a stronghold of conservative and bourgeois culture. In a way, the Dagmar Theatre became the place where popular culture and high culture met and mingled. In this fashion, it was here and in other commercial theatres, such as the Casino, and not at the Royal Theatre that new impulses from abroad first were encountered. Ibsen, Bjørnson, and a number of contemporary female playwrights got widely played at the Dagmar.[14]

Did this mean that the Royal Theatre was entirely supassed by other theatres? Not in every respect. After the inauguration of the new building in

1874, a number of modern technical devices were introduced and in the following years, electrical stage lighting was widely installed as well as sophisticated stage machinery.[15] The Royal Theatre also staged most of Ibsen's plays shortly after they were written and mostly before they were published.[16]

A loser

Bjørnson, Ibsen, and Strindberg were rather successful in Paris in the 1890s, but there is also a reverse of the medal. Not every Scandinavian playwright did as well as those three and some of them were plain losers in their efforts to establish themselves on the Parisian stage. Especially after 1897, the 'blizzard from the North' seems to have lost its power as suddenly as it had appeared, and the tide for foreign drama turned.

One of the playwrights that did not make it in Paris was the Dane, Holger Drachmann, although he did his very best to win distinction there. One of the badly concealed aims of Drachmann's urge to conquer Paris was that, in doing so, he hoped to surpass both Ibsen and Strindberg. Drachmann was, during most of his lifetime, constantly striving to become and to stay Denmark's most important living author. Living by his pen, Drachmann had to keep in touch with the 'market' by constantly attracting publicity, a thing he managed to do with remarkable skill. For the great Scandinavian authors, it was necessary to keep an eye on the competition, especially when international fame was involved. We know, for example, that Strindberg kept a close look at how the other Scandinavians were received by foreign audiences and critics, afraid as he was of having to stand in someone else's shadow.[17]

Notwithstanding Drachmann's great fame, he was rapidly forgotten after his death. Whether or not he was inspired by the fortune of Ibsen, Bjørnson, and Strindberg and their huge successes abroad, he also started writing drama in the the the mid-1880's. Drachmann's dramatical *oeuvre* culminated in 1894, when he wrote the first two of a series of melodrama's.[18] Nearly all of these melodramas are, seen from a modern perspective, on the wrong side of the borderline between good and bad taste. Drachmann has, in a sense, become a pitiful figure and, today, his plays are largely forgotten.

Drachmann wrote melodrama in order to make a separate niche for himself and, thus, he had to develop new aspects of the melodramatic genre, sometimes coming close to the Wagnerian *Gesamtkunstwerk*. His plays are an exotic mixture of styles and forms, in which costumes, text, acting, and music are amalgamated. As a matter of fact, he developed the melodramatic genre as a result of the ever-growing need for success that originated, among other things, from his bad financial situation.[19] The moving force behind writing melodramas was that they were *en vogue* and that they would provided him with extra income. Drachmann was very well aware of the new economic opportunities that the stage could offer in the 1890s, because he himself had been a member of a committee that formulated the new rules for dividing the box-office takings between theatres, actors, and writers.[20] As one of the very few Danish professional authors who lived exclusively by his pen, Drachmann was highly dependent on 'the market', especially his publisher Hegel. This dependence forced him to write at a great rate and in vastly different genres.[21]

When Drachmann himself was in Paris in 1901, he wrote to his Danish publisher, Jacob Hegel:

> This week my friend Armand Point has been in Paris and read half of "Vølund" to his literary friends. Great excitement. Not since the days of Victor Hugo — so they say — has such poetry been heard in France. (...) They are writing articles on me — people are making pilgrimages to me — in 5-6 weeks Armand and I hope to have the translation finished — then we will look for a theatre in Paris — and in Brussels — and, in short, I am working assiduously at competing with Bjørnson and Ibsen on the market place of "world fame". (Borup 1970: 150; transl.: W. Glyn Jones)

However, the above mentioned melodrama, *Vølund Smed* (1894), was never performed, either in Paris or Brussels. Drachmann tried to conquer Paris at a moment when Scandinavian theatre was out of fashion and, as a matter of fact, with a dramatic genre that was waning to its (literary) close. Outwardly, even while writing to his life-long publisher, Drachmann had to present himself as the great creator of timeless and priceless masterpieces, while at the same time he was well aware that he was in decline. His health became poorer by the day, his debts kept increasing, and there did not appear to be much prospect of world fame, however hard he fought for it.[22] Not even his last desperate move, writing a number of melodramas and other plays, could correct the situation.

On the occasion of Drachmann's 60th birthday, he was honoured by the Royal Theater, which performed the last play he was to write, *Hr. Oluf han rider* (1906), and as an omen of his fading star, this play was a disaster. The performance was, even by sympathetic critics, characterized as "a first rate festive flop".[23]

In this response to Egil Törnqvist's paper I have drawn attention to the role of Herman Bang as mediator of Scandinavian theatre in Paris, to the importance of the Parisian political context of the mid-1890s in which the Scandinavian plays were staged and received, and I have taken a closer look at the situation in Danish theatre around the year 1894, with particular attention to Holger Drachmann. All are significant and at the same time just minor elements, in the kaleidoscopic complexity of European theatre of the mid-1890s, a veritable period of turmoil.

Notes

1. *Trætte Mænd* (1891), German translation: *Müde Seelen* (1893).

2. See Fischer, 1978, pp. 29-33.

3. Examples of authors that lived abroad during most of their carreer are the Norwegian writer and playwright, Amalie Skram (1846-1905), who settled down in Copenhagen in the early 1880s, but kept writing in Norwegian, and Icelandic writers such as Jóhann Sigurjónsson (1880-1919), who lived in Copenhagen from the mid-1890s onward. One of the rare exceptions is the Swedish painter Ivan Aguéli (1869-1917), who did not return to Sweden and even adopted a new name.

4. According to Hanne Amsinck, Edvard Munch and Knut Hamsun had also lived in this boarding-house in the early 1890's. See Amsinck, 1972, p. 23.

5. Amsinck, p. 42, states that this implies an average production of not less than 4 to 5 articles a day.

6. See Amsinck, 1972, p. 21.

7. In 1901 Tailhade was convicted and imprisoned because he wrote an article advocating the assassination of the Russian Czar during a visit to France. See Ahlström, 1956, pp. 216, 219; Woodcock, 1975, p. 91; as well as Quack, 1977, p. 350, note 1.

8. Woodcock, p. 91.

9. Fischer, pp. 46-47.

10. Amsinck, p. 18.

11. See Christensen, 1989, pp. 9-19.

12. The Tivoli Gardens were established in 1843 and in 1874 also got a theatre.

13. Some of the most interesting examples are female writers, in the 1890s notably Karen Bramson and Amalie Skram. See Jensen, 1984, pp. 9-33.

14. Strindberg wanted to stage *Miss Julie* at the Dagmar Theatre in March 1889, but was prevented by the official theatre censor. Subsequently it was performed for a closed audience in the Copenhagen Student Society and thereafter publicly played in Paris at the Théâtre Libre in 1893.

15. See: "Bag Tæppet" by Jul. Lehmann, in: Hansen 1889-1896, Vol. 3, pp. 429-456.

16. The breaking-point was *Ghosts*, which was rejected by the Royal Theatre in 1881. See Kela Kvam, 1992, Vol.2, p. 76.

17. Ahlström 1956, pp. 198-199.

18. These first two melodramas are *Vølund Smed* and *Renæssance*.

19. See my article "'Take here a glimpse of former times". On Holger Drachmann's historical melodramas *Vølund Smed* and *Renæssance*', in *Scandinavica* Vol. 33 (1994), Nr. 2.

20. This commission was called *Theater-Regulativ Kommissionen*, installed 31. august 1889. See Hansen, Vol. 3, p. 278.

21. According to Torben Kragh Grodal, in *Dansk litteraturhistorie*, this meant that for an author like Drachmann "in order to have a decent middle-class existence, it was necessary to get to seven publications a year, write sales successes or supplement his other work with journalism, readings, lectures and translations. (...) The disproportion between income and expenditure made authors dependent on the publishers, who by means of advance payments, financed authors working regularly for them." In: Busk-Jensen 1985, Vol. 6, p. 357.

22. He was left out when the first Nobel Prize for Literature was awarded in 1901, and was nominated in vain in later years.

23. Neiiendam 1948, p. 202 states: "Ringe Glæde fik den store Lyriker af sit sidste Skuespil, den danske Sommernats Drama *Hr. Oluf, han rider*, som opførtes paa Digterens 60 Aarsdag i 1906, men som med Einar Christiansens Ord blev 'en Festfiasco af Rang', hvortil ogsaa Udførelsen bidrog."

References

Ahlström, Stellan, *Strindbergs erövring av Paris*. Stockholm: Almqvist & Wiksell, 1956.

Amsinck, Hanne, *Sceneinstruktøren Herman Bang og det franske symbolistiske teater*. Copenhagen: G.E.C. Gads Forlag, 1972.

Andersen, Per Thomas, *Dekadanse i nordisk litteratur 1880-1900*. Oslo: Aschehoug, 1992.

Borup, Morten (red.), *Breve fra og til Holger Drachmann* I-IV. Copenhagen: Gyldendal, 1970.

Busk-Jensen, Lise (et al.), *Dansk litteratur historie* 6. Copenhagen: Gyldendal, 1985.

Christensen, Erik M., *Henrik Ibsens anarkisme: de samle værker* 1-2. Copenhagen: Akademisk Forlag, 1989.

Drachmann, Holger, *Poetiske Skrifter*. Copenhagen: Gyldendal, 1927.

Fischer, Jens Malte, *Fin de siècle. Kommentar zu einer Epoche*. Munich: Winkler Verlag, 1978.

Hansen, P., *Den danske Skueplads. Illustreret Theaterhistorie* 1-3. Copenhagen: Ernst Bojesens Kunstforlag, 1889-1896.

Ibsen, Henrik, *Samlede værker*. Oslo: Gyldendal Norsk Forlag, 1952. (10th edition by Didrik Arup Seip)

Jensen, Astrid, 'Ibsens og Strindbergs søstre'. In: Astrid Jensen (et al.). *Teatrets Kvinder*. Gråsten: Drama, 1984, pp. 9-33.

Kvam, Kela (red. e.a.), *Dansk Teaterhistorie* 1-2. Copenhagen: Gyldendal, 1992.

Lauring, Palle, *Ej blot til lyst. Det kongelige teater 1874-1974*. Copenhagen: Forum, 1974.

Leicht, Georg & Marianne Hallar, *Det kongelige Teaters repertoire 1889-1975*. Copenhagen: Biblioteks-centralens Forlag, 1977.

Liet, Henk van der, '"Take here a fleeting glimpse of former times." On Holger Drachmann's historical melodramas *Vølund Smed* and *Renæssance*.' In: *Scandinavica* 33 (1994), nr. 2.

Neiiendam, Robert, *Det kongelige Teaters Historie 1890-1892*. Copenhagen: Selskabet for Dansk Teaterhistorie, 1970.

Neiiendam, Robert, 'Det realistiske Teater.' In: Alf Henriques (et al.). *Teatret paa Kongens Nytorv 1748-1948*. Copenhagen: Berlingske Forlag, 1948, pp. 175-216.

Quack. H.P.G., *De socialisten* 6. Baarn: Het Wereldvenster, 1977.

Rubow, Paul V., *Holger Drachmann. Sidste aar*. Copenhagen: Ejnar Munksgaards Forlag, 1950.

Strindberg, August, *Skrifter*. Stockholm: Albert Bonniers Förlag, 1945. (edited and annotated by Gunnar Brandell).

Woodcock, George, *Anarchism. A History of Libertarian Ideas and movements*. Harmondsworth: Penguin Books, 1975.

107

Christa Hasche
'REVUE OR THEATRE': ON SOME ASPECTS OF THE CHANGE
IN FUNCTION OF THEATRE IN BERLIN CIRCA 1894, WITH
REFERENCE TO THE ESTABLISHMENT OF A CITY REVUE THEATRE

To limit this discussion to the centre of Berlin is in fact to focus on the decisive developments for the whole of Germany at the turn of the century. At that time Berlin's development as a metropolis and world city took off at a rate previously unknown. The emergence of the industrial city was shaped by a dynamic of change whose virulent pace of growth affected all spheres of life. Such a radical change in the way of life with the associated social and topographical rejections, differentiations, forced deculturalisations etc. are relevant here in terms of the formation of an urban subjectivity as characterised by certain layers of the upper and middle classes and reflected by artists and intellectuals.

Particularly conspicuous is a keen awareness and renewed approach regarding the scale of space, time and movement. The historian Karl Lamprecht describes the contemporary experience thus:

> Der deutsche Großkaufmann des 18. Jahrhunderts und der ersten Hälfte des 19. Jahrhunderts der am ehesten noch als Vorgänger der modernen industriellen, kommerziellen und finanziellen Schichten der Unternehmung anzusprechen ist, war (...) ein behäbiger Herr; mit geröteten Wangen sah er unter seiner Perücke oder aus seinem Vatermörder in die Welt; jovial, behaglich, seiner Stellung und der Anerkennung seines Berufes, der in der Dichtung der Zeit so oft gepriesenen 'Handlung', sicher...Wie anders fühlen wir!...Wir sind die Kinder einer anderen Zeit, geistig und körperlich hart und straff gebaut, (...) dem Sachlichen zugewandt, bisweilen mit vor lauter Sachlichkeit inhaltsleeren Zügen; wir blicken wohl in stillen Stunden in die Vergangenheit der letzten anderthalb Jahrhunderte wie in ein verlorenes Paradies zurück, doch ihm angehört zu haben würde kaum in unseren Wünschen liegen: denn vorwärts ohne Rast lautet das Wahlwort der Gegenwart, und zeitlos wäre, wer den Genuß eines nimmermüden Fortschrittes für das Linsengericht einer quietistisch erscheinenden Vergangenheit dahingäbe (...) was dabei aus unserem Empfinden spricht (...) das ist die Seele des heutigen deutschen Bürgertums an führender Stelle, ist der Geist der Unternehmung.[1]

This affirmative attitude, expressly faithful in progress, as well as of radical cultural change appears to underlie the continuing advancement. Lamprecht continues:

> Was also den modernen Zeitbegriff zunächst kennzeichnet, das ist die genaue praktische Beachtung des kleinen Zeitabschnittes: Fünfminu-

tenaudienzen, Minutengespräche am Telephon, Sekunden-produktion der Rotationsdruckmaschine, Fünftelsekundenmessung beim Fahrrad (...) Zugleich aber ist damit der Sinn für das, was Zeit ist und sich an Zeit messen läßt, überhaupt gewachsen; leichter als früheren Zeitaltern wird uns auch die Vorstellung größerer Zeiträume (...) man kann die Erziehung zu einer neuen Raumanschauung geradezu einen der wesentlichen Vorgänge des geistigen Bildungsprozesses der jüngsten Vergangenheit bezeichnen. Das was hier durch den neuen Verkehr zunächst geweckt wurde, war das Gefühl gleichsam der Allgegenwart auf Erden.[2]

Within the urban context, the newly available cultural opportunities served to develop the consciousness of the economically mobile bourgeoisie. Georg Simmel has described this as "nervousness" in relation to the assimilation of "rapid crowding together of changing images, from within the wide margins of that which one can take in with one look, to the unexpectedness of forced impressions."[3]
The young Gerhart Hauptmann (whose *Weber* was premiered at the Deutsches Theater in 1894), vividly described the overwhelming first impression which Berlin first made on him.

Zum ersten Mal empfand ich Rhythmus, Rausch und Wogengärung der großen Stadt. Die Wirkung war sinnbetäubend und fortreißend. Ohne sich selbst aufzugeben, konnte man meinen, keine Eigenbewegung zu haben, sondern ein vom großen Ganzen bewegte Monade zu sein (...) Unsere erste Wohnung lag im vierten Stock eines Moabiter Wohnhauses. Die Aussicht war frei über die Berliner Stadtbahn hinweg und den ausgedehnten Güterbahnhof. Fast ununterbrochen donnerten Züge vorüber (...) Der Berliner Puls war erregend und fortreißend. Besonders die Anforderungen an den Gehörsinn durch den unablässigen Stadtbahndonner waren ungeheuerlich.[4]

Fragmentation, rhythmicality and rapid changes of perspective are the constituent elements of this fresh city consciousness, a city which underwent a media revolution owing to electrification (transport: 1895 the first electrical tramway rode in Berlin, it was tested as early as 1881), advertising and photography, all of which changed cultural communication fundamentally. Traditional art forms, genres and techniques were put to the test and were unable to withstand the change.

Man kann einen Roman schreiben von 200 Seiten und er ist vortrefflich. Man kann dasselbe auf 3 Seiten sagen und es ist ebenso vortrefflich. Das Ganze ist eine Zeitersparnis. Es gibt heutzutage viele sonst tüchtige Menschen, die keine Zeit haben 200 Seiten zu lesen. Diesen gibt man 3 Seiten im Extrakte.[5]

The city dweller also desired a new theatre. According to O.J. Bierbaum:

> Der heutige Stadtmensch hat, wenn Sie Gütigste das gewagte Wort
> erlauben, Varieténerven; er hat nur noch selten die Fähigkeit großen
> dramatischen Zusammenhängen zu folgen, sein Empfindungsleben für
> drei Theaterstunden auf einen Ton zu stimmen; er will Abwechslung,
> — Varieté.[6]

Variety in place of theatre! No three-hour dramatic correlations in view of the
one-fifth of a second measures, for three hours all the senses tuned to a
single note; that is unthinkable for the 'nervous modern'. It is not simply a
question of the rejection of this or the other theatre.
'Revue or theatre' is the title of an essay by Walter Benjamin and Bernhard
Reich from 1925 which I have borrowed here. The date testifies: the issue
remains 'unsolved'. Interestingly, in their critique, Benjamin and Reich also
refer to the foundations laid by the cultural historical revolution of the 90's,
and make the point:

> Das Theater ist ein Theater der vergangenen Epochen geblieben, es
> entspricht in der Planheit der Kleinstaaterei, in den Problemen der
> Seelenzergliederung dem Müßiggang, der aller Laster Anfang ist, in
> seinem Theaterbau der Kammerspieldiele, der Beschränktheit seiner
> Insassen, in seinen dünnen, sich langsam realisierenden Beziehungen
> einer Zeit, in der die Postkutsche das modernste Verkehrsmittel war
> (...) Zwischen der Revue und den Phantasiekräften der Bewohner der
> großen Städte steht wehrend der Kordon der Bildungstrabanten, unter
> ihnen der Dichter (...) Die Revue hat es nicht nötig, im scheuen Bogen
> um das vom Dichter besetzte Gebiet herumzugehen, sie mag ganz
> frech eindringen! Die feierliche Kontinuität der Akte, die uns nichts
> erspart, aber nur kleine Territorien bestreicht, können wir uns nicht
> leisten.[7]

In view of the circumstances of communication created by the city, the
existing theatre seemed outmoded. In the concepts presented here, the model
of theatre assumed is the traditional form which dominated since the
Renaissance through to the 18th century, and which sprung from the
dominance of literary expression and from fully-fledged works of art.
(Further aspects such as mimetic talent will not be detailed here). The
conception and practice of a revue theatre was also instrumental in the
re-framing of theatre at the turn of the century. In his interpretation, Jochen
Fiebach claims that during this revolutionary period 'before the First World
War' attention was sharply focussed at particular intervals:

> Auf das neue Verständnis von Kunst vor allem als einem Feld
> entfesselbarer, letztlich unbegrenzter Kreativität; als einem Bereich, in
> dem ganz eigenartige andere Welten oder eben Realitäten imaginativ

konstruiert werden können, und auf das radikale Interesse für die
Sinnlichkeiten, für die Gestalten und Formen, daher auch gerade für
die Überflächen der Existenzen. Das galt in besonderem Maße für den
Umgang mit Kunst.[8]

It is necessary to return specifically to this final point. First some decisive
economic changes must be pointed out. Theatre became institutionalised as
a commercial entity with the extension of free trade to this sphere in 1869. In
practical terms this meant an effective end to the bourgeois national theatre
ideology (viewing the theatre as a centre of education, a temple, a national
consecration space.)

The foundation of commercial theatre enabled various layers of the
bourgeoisie and middle classes freely to signal their theatre requirements as
such, in terms of content, function, methods of communication and form.

Alone the number of theatres established in this period bears testimony to
this. (I leave out the problematic of the granting of licences, the continual
bankruptcies, the proletisation of stage personnel etc.) In 1897 Berlin boasted
35 theatres with a total capacity of circa 43 000 seats.[9] This does not include
the attendance at the many theatre societies (including the Volksbühne). As
a comparison: between 1871 and 1900 the population of Berlin increased from
825 000 to 1 889 000.[10] This growing number of theatres competed by means
of specialization. Already in the 70s, the decade of unlimited theatrical
freedom, Berlin theatre had developed a distinctive profile. The Friedrich-
Wilhelm Städtisches Theatre was the leading operetta theatre in Berlin, the
Wallner theatre provided local farce, the Krollsche theatre was famous for its
summer opera, and there was theatre for the holidays: magic as well as
vaudeville.[11]

One among these many theatres, the Central Theatre had developed the
Berlin farce into an "international farce spectacular" (J.Bab) as from 1880.[12] In
his essay "The theatre stage as as popular institution" the critic and literary
theorist Paul Schlenther remarks as early as 1885 on a particular feature of
this theatre:

> Herr Ernst [d.i. Adolf Ernst, Direktor, Ch.H.] kommt mit der eigenen
> Schauspielerei so wenig über ein bescheidenes Mittelmaß hinaus, wie
> die meisten seiner Mitwirkenden; der Kunstgriff aber, womit er die
> Massen zwingt, ist das schnelle Tempo, der flotte Zug und eine den
> Grundton an stimmende liebenswürdige Selbstironie (...).[13]

In 1893, this theatre opened with the revue 'Berlin 1893', a series of yearly
revues which were new for Berlin, and above all were marked out by their
topicality and stage set effects:

> Das erste Bild zeigte den Stadtbahnbogen am Bahnhof Friedrich-straße
> (...) das zweite Bild den neuen Reichstag (...) Zweifellos den Höhe-
> punkt (...) bildete aber das 3. Bild (...) Es wurde eine 'lebensgetreue

Wiedergabe der Hubertusjagd' gezeigt. Nach dem Muster der Londoner Bühnen war eine 'landschaftlich schöne Partie des Grüne-walds, wie sie in Wirklichkeit ist' dargestellt, mit echtem Moosteppich, plastischen Baumstämmen, 'wirklichen Blättern und Sträuchern'. Nichts war gemalt.[14]

As with the sets, 'real' effects were sought for in the cast.

(...) brachte sie [die Regie, Ch.H.] (...) sogar 'original italienische Straßensänger, Dudelsackpfeiffer und Tänzerinnen', die in der italieni-schen Ausstellung aufgetreten waren auf die Bühne. Und im 6. Bild traten neben der echten ungarischen Nationalkapelle (...) auch 8-10 Mädchen auf, die sich Schultz aus den 'Blumensälen' geholt hatte.[15]

This demonstrates the fascination with the surface of appearances, for the sense of the material, which appears to have been barely aesthetically reduced. This sensory reflection appears to be a naive materialist self-affirma-tion of acquired wealth. The revue theatre was a site unifying the interests of the newly self-confident professional classes with their demand for a particular kind of entertainment, towards a culture which is actually now considered modern, with the conceptions of the reformers (e.g. Behrens, Fuchs), in spite of theatrical artistic expectations being light years apart. The emphasis on 'real' effects, their authenticity which should testify to the exciting cultural activity of the city, refers back (also in the value of sensation) to the regular educational theatre as well as older forms of entertainment in terms of these requirements. Sensory pleasure rather than depth of meaning, experience rather than discourse (H. Müller) seems to be the foundation of this theatre. A valid interpretation, which is often enough presented through the exclusive interpretation of any high art which is understood on the level of 'depth of meaning'.

In the 90's it was principally the Metropole Theatre in Berlin which developed a profile enabling theatre to be understood as a gregarious space and international meeting point for cosmopolitan people. In this respect the theatre building was of greatest significance. The theatre in Behrenstrasse, completed in 1892 (today the Komische Oper, Ch.H.) was designed to suit the target audience, to meet the social requirements of the Berlin set:

(...) des hatte eine Million und dreihunderttausend Mark gekostet, und das sah man (...) die Parkettlogen und Ränge waren nicht abge-schlossen, sondern sie eröffneten sich ohne trennende Mauern gegen die mahagoniegetäfelten Umgänge mit ihren Polstersesseln und Tischen, wo man ausgezeichnet speisen oder Champagner trinken konnte. Geraucht werden durfte überall (...).[16]

Even the outer rooms delineated a theatre of convivial entertainment, of diffusion, in which a multitude of pleasures would be facilitated and into which the stage production had to find its place. No secret was made of the fact that art was not the exclusive raison d'etre for this cultural experience. This break from the traditional role of theatre as an educational institution, an "educational satellite concern" (as Benjamin/Reich described it) was keenly defended against accusations of "city amusement business" (a "circus agent for jobbers", "a vulgar educational institution") which came from the more idealized folklore interests:

> Sie [das Publikum, Ch.H.] wirbeln in den Pausen durcheinander, sie wispern und flirten mit den schönen Freundinnen, sie machen Meinung für und wider, und zwischen ihnen steht verraten und verkauft der ernste und gewissenhafte Kritiker, der nicht weiß, ob er die Dinge ernst oder auf die leichte Achsel nehmen soll. Ganz entschieden das letztere, meine Herren! Eine Revue (...) will geschlürft werden wie prickelnder französischer Sekt, als eine heitere Stunde flüchtigen Genusses, an die man mit heitrem Lächeln und einem kleinen Schuß erotischen Behagens gern zurückdenkt (...).[17]

The Metropole Theatre was widely known for its yearly revue in particular (a form which was nurtured from the 90's up until the First World War, but which, superseded by the Americanization of the revue, was not taken up again.) Six-figure sums for a production were not uncommon:

> In diesen echten Jahresrevuen fanden alle irgendwie zu szenischer Wirkung geeigneten jüngsten Begebenheiten der Politik, der Kunst, der Gerichtssäle und der Gesellschaft, vermischt mit volkstümlichen Typen (...) ihre satirische oder possenhafte Verwertung. Eine wesentliche Grundlage für den Erfolg war es, daß man auf die differenzierten Geschmacksrichtungen eines vielfältigen Publikums einzugehen verstand. Für den Feinschmecker fanden sich immer Szenen literarischen Charakters, und den Durchschnitt befriedigten derb-komische, possenhafte Auftritte, melodiöse Lieder (...) Das Ganze war in den Rahmen einer bis dahin nicht gekannten Ausstattungspracht gestellt, deren Reiz noch durch das Aufgebot vieler schöner Frauen gewann.[18]

Musicalization, visualization and an increase in sexual appeal were the aesthetic hallmarks of these revues. The female body was introduced as an integral part of the fascination with surface appearances. In the 90's the female body was introduced on stage as part of the 'corps de ballet'.

> In historischen Uniformen ziehen die alten preussischen Regimenter zum großen Zapfenstreich auf, mit kriegerischen Trommeln und Fanfaren, eine hübsche Parade, die mancher einer wirklichen auf dem Tempelhofer Felde vorziehen wird. Denn was hier paradiert, sind die tadellosen Beine des weiblichen Chorpersonals.[19]

It was precisely the pure exhibition of physicality which made this kind of ostensibily random projection area possible, in this case via the glorification of the Prussian military, where in fact the female body specifically remained the specialization for surface appearance. Some subjects of the revue demonstrate nicely the connection between 'femininity and metropolis', a stock theme in rhetoric also within other genres before and at the turn of the century. (Sigrid Weigel has drawn attention to the function of the feminine.) The following extract from the revue *Der Teufel lacht dazu* offers an example of the sexualisation and feminization of the city as metaphor:[20]

> Die Hölle eine lustige, urfidele Hölle mit Teufelinnen in verdammt lüsternen Seidentrikots, eine Hölle in der unaufhörlich gesungen, getanzt und gewitzelt wird (...) Seine höllische Majestät (...) hat eine große Audienz gegeben für alle Sündengesandtinnen, die der Teufel in den großen Städten unterhält. Die Sünde von Berlin macht ihre Reverenz. Er ist mit ihren Leistungen nicht zufrieden. In Berlin wird ihm nicht genügend gesündigt. Satan beschließt in höchst eigener Person nach dem Rechten zu sehen und selbst nach Berlin zu fahren. Nun sehen wir im 2. Bild mit der Sünde von Berlin auf seiner Teufelsfahrt.[21]

This is simultaneously a play on female allegory, which is consciously opposed to the virtuous depictions made in the public arena. The revues before the First World War do show a great affinity to allegorical presentations. There are several reasons for this, but it is most significantly made possible by the availibility/formation of a relatively closed upper class, and the production of a common horizon of understanding which affirmed and helped create these revues. Beyond this, the revue form had a certain affinity with allegorical presentations in terms of attention to the sensory, and the visual quality of the material. Finally we find the standardisation of female roles, such as the star, but also the role of ballet girl, which was modernised in the 20s into the 'girl'.

> (...) hüpft ein flottes, liebes Mädel auf die Bühne, das Mädel vom Metropol. Es hat mit einem Grafen ein kleines Intermezzo.[22]

On June 16th 1898, reflecting on a 10 year period of rule, the Kaiser expressed his thanks to the Berlin Royal Theatre for their support for his cultural programme: "(...) in the belief in God to serve the spirit of idealism and to continue the struggle against materialism and all which is un-German, to which unfortunately some German stages have fallen (...) that all nations are closely observing the activities of the royal theatre and look on with amazement (...) both points of view originate from a lamentable self-deception."[22]

The complete closure of the royal theatres, the completion of the notion of the national theatre and compulsory movement towards specialisation, the revue theatre had proved itself immensely suitable as theatre form. The development of the citizens-revue in Berlin at the turn of the century occurred in close connection with the development of the city itself and the inevitable radical change in cultural communication as well as the endeavour to achieve bourgeois society entertainment worthy of a world city. The pace of life could be matched by this theatrical form. Thereby both the wealth and the way of life of the founding bourgeoisie were represented. Most importantly, since the turn of the century the revue theatre modernised and orientated itself to the tastes of upper class entertainment and representation. It defined itself as a gregarious social space and topical event, introduced by means of multi-layered sensual pleasure, ostentatiously rejecting educational practice. The popular revue theatre of the "anti-naturalistic revolution" at the turn of the century worked through the re-discovery and modernisation of the revue via the secularization of the theatre, the primacy of its showbiz character and its de-literification (text for actual use). 'Reception in diffusion' (Benjamin) lifted this revue theatre to a modern form.

Notes

1. Karl Lamprecht, *Deutsche Geschichte. Zur jüngsten deutschen Vergangenheit* (Freiburg, 1903). Vol. 2, part 1, pp. 241-2.

2. *Ibidem*: 159. See also Bernd Schmidt, *Die Dynamisierung des Kommunikations- und Verkehrsrhythmus als kultureller Massenprozeß in Berlin 1880-1914 und Aspekte seiner Relevanz in den darstellenden Künsten.* Phil. Diss. Berlin, 1990.

3. Georg Simmel, 'Die Großstädte und das Geistesleben.' In: Schutte, Jürgen and Peter Sprengel (eds.). *Die Berliner Moderne 1885-1914* (Stuttgart, 1987), pp. 124-5.

4. Gerhart Hauptmann, *Die Weber* (Berlin, 1980), pp. 471-593.

5. Peter Altenberg, *Bilderbögen des kleinen Lebens* (Berlin 1909), p. 164.

6. Otto Julius Bierbaum in: Hamann, H. and J. Hermand, *Impressionismus* (Berlin, 1960), p. 146.

7. Walter Benjamin and Bernhard Reich. 'Revue oder Theater.' In: *Der Querschnitt* (Berlin, 1925), p. 1039.

8. Joachim Fiebach, *Von Craigh bis Brecht* (Berlin 1991), p. 50.

9. Max Martersteig, *Das deutsche Theater im neunzehnten Jahrhundert* (Leipzig, 1924), p. 698.

10. Paul Linsemann, 'Die Theaterstadt Berlin.' In: *Theateralmanach von 1897* (Berlin, 1897), Anhang.

11. Jürgen Kuczynski, *Geschichte des Alltags des deutschen Volkes* (Berlin, 1982), Vol. 4, p. 206.

12. Rita Klis, *Anspruch der deutschen Bourgeoisie auf ein ihr gemäßes Theater und Versuche seiner Realisierung (1870-1880)*. Phil.Diss. Berlin 1980, pp. 55ff.

13. Paul Schlenther, 'Die Schaubühne als volkstümliche Anstalt betrachtet.' In: *Die Nation* 2, nr. 43, p. 1885.

14. Peter Windelboth, *Das Central-Theater in Berlin 1880-1908*. Phil.Diss. Berlin 1956, pp. 219ff.

15. *Ibidem*, p. 219.

16. Otto Schneidereit, *Berlin wie es weint und lacht* (Berlin, 1973), pp. 212-3.

17. Walter Freund, 'Aus der Frühzeit des Berliner Metropoltheater.' In: *Kleine Schriften der Gesellschaft für Theatergeschichte* 19 (Berlin 1962), p. 48.

18. Rudolph Nelson and Julius Freund, *Chauffeur, ins Metropol. Große Jahresrevue mit Gesang und Tanz in 10 Bildern*. Berlin, Ed. Note & Bock, pp. 50-1.

19. Otto Schneidereit, *Op.cit.*, p. 125.

20. Sigrid Weigel, 'Die Städte sind weiblich und nur dem Sieger hold. Zur Funktion des Weiblichen in Gründungsmythen und Städtedarstellungen.' In: Anselm, S. and B. Beck (eds.). *Triumph und Scheitern in der Metropole. Zur Rolle der Weiblichkeit in der Geschichte Berlins*. Berlin: Reimer, 1987.

21. Otto Schneidereit, *Op.cit.*, p. 122.

22. *Ibidem*, p. 124.

Karel Hupperetz
THEATRE INSTEAD OF REVUE

Christa Hasche's text, 'Revue or Theatre', is an extremely fascinating attempt to add to the traditional picture of theatre in and around 1894 through an analysis of the revue. Her account enriches the overall panorama of theatre in the nineteenth century.

My contribution mainly focuses on the phenomenon of the panorama as a metaphor for the richly varied picture of theatre at this time. Moreover, the panorama can also be regarded as one of the main examples of spectacular amusement for the masses, side by side with the more popular form of theatre called the revue.[1]

Of course, on a superficial level the panorama is a specifically pictorial genre, but from the spectator's point of view there are certainly parallels with the theatrical subgenres from the nineteenth century. The panorama with its huge painting, with its 'fauxterrain' — a kind of middle ground or proscenium containing pieces of scenery and functioning as a transitional area for the spectators on the platform — was considered a form of Art which played with the illusion of reality. With its suggestive tricks, optical illusions, sensational effects and enchantments, the panorama entertained and at the same time catered to an audience that craved images. To a nineteenth-century audience, the panorama was an expression of the dream of a large space; an attempt to show the entirety of a real event instead of a mere fragment.

In the nineteenth century, the panorama was one of the main forms of spectator amusement via its presentation of the illusion of reality. In the same way as in the theatrical subgenres of the nineteenth century, the traditional perspective of the court theatres was also transcended in the panorama. Painters no longer adopted the central perspective of the sovereign, as it was no longer necessary to present a feudal power. The panorama was a poly-perspective and democratic art form, but at the same time it was of course only compensatory from the point of view of the spectator, as — in contrast to the theatrical genres — it always lacked the immediate physical sensorial experience; the performance by real people. In her lecture, Christa Hasche applies the dimensions of space, time and movement — the 'Allgegenwart' in terms of Lamprecht, whom she quotes — to the revue. It could be argued that these dimensions are present in the panorama in a very specific way. The panorama combined history, the existing political situation and the needs of the spectators in a deceptively realistic way. It presented an overall picture, whilst in actual life people are only ever able to perceive fragments of reality. On the other hand, the panorama broke with the traditionally privileged forms of art, which had always permitted only a small minority to decode the mythological imagery used.

Through its precision and totality, the panorama attempted to come to grips with a historical or natural event, in the same way as the great historians of the nineteenth century did. Mommsen, for example, tried to present a complete history of Rome, Michelet of the French Revolution. They wanted to show 'wie es eigentlich gewesen'. In the novel (the linguistic counterpart of the visual panorama) Zola, for example, tried to present a complete review of his time in *Les Rougon-Macquart*. In the same way, the Meiningers attempted to conjure up the real illusion of Schiller's *Wilhelm Tell* or Shakespeare's *Julius Caesar* in their productions of these plays. Equally, in the panorama, dynamics, movement and precision replaced the traditional and more static way of painting. In the course of time, the panorama then developed by way of the diorama to a panorama of motion — to film — when the images learned to move. It can therefore be said that this democratic, earliest visual mass medium, one that had existed for more than a century, ultimately gave way to the new media of the twentieth century.

After this brief introduction I would like to make some comments on the similarities and differences between the revue and other theatrical subgenres, as well as on the great influence of foreign developments on them. Historically speaking, French *variété* and *Café-chantant* and English *Music Hall*, with their short, snappy, scanty scenic structures, certainly influenced the revue. Because of its concentration on Berlin as the cultural metropolis, at least the two other German-speaking cultural centres in the period around 1894, Munich and Vienna keep out of the picture. The entire period at the end of the nineteenth century was characterized by a great variety of styles and genres, by a 'Gleichzeitigkeit des Ungleichzeitigen'.
As far as Berlin is concerned, the group of naturalists around the *Durch*-society should certainly be highlighted, as well as the important role of the stimulator Otto Brahm, the writer Gerhard Hauptmann, the eminent role of the *Freie Bühne* (where on 26 February 1893, for example, one of the central naturalistic texts, *Die Weber*, was first staged), the *Freie Volksbühne* and the *Deutsches Theater* (where the first public performance of *Die Weber* was given on 25 September 1894). The work of the naturalists, besides the revue and the *variété*, besides the epigonic *Klassik*, the romantic *Konsumliteratur* and the affirmative bourgeois culture, marked the beginning of a new way of writing, a new dramaturgy, a different way of acting and staging plays, the search for new audiences. With its circle around Conrad and *Die Gesellschaft*, Munich harboured the precursors of the naturalists, but it was also the city of *Einzelgänger* such as Wedekind, who wrote *Die Büchse der Pandora* (the forerunner of *Lulu*), or Oskar Panizza, who published his offensive play *Das Liebeskonzil* in 1894. In Vienna, the Café Griensteidl formed an early centre of symbolism, with a group around Hermann Bahr, Arthur Schnitzler and Hugo von Hofmannsthal, whose *Der Tor und der Tod* was published in Munich in 1893 in the *Moderne Musenalmanach auf das Jahr 1894*.
Each way of limiting the study of this period to one or the other specific subject is at the expense of a sufficient light on the exciting, highly complex 'Gleichzeitigkeit des Ungleichzeitigen'. The *Lexikon der Künste* included in the programme accompanying the performance of Wedekind's *Die Büchse der Pandora* by the theatre company from Erlangen (pp. 85-117)[2] attests this inter-

national and complex character of the period. A quotation from the introduction: "1894, also genau hundert Jahre vor uns, ist nahe genug, um den Aufbruch ins plurale 20. Jahrhundert schon anzeigen zu können. Die Kunst der Moderne faltet sich auf in viele Stile..." (p. 7).

Christa Hasche's lecture links the abolishment of the *Gewerbegesetze* in 1869 to the movement away from the traditional, bourgeois *Nationaltheater* ideology. All things considered, this is of course correct, but at the same time it caused a gigantic explosion of new theatres and fierce competition. From that moment on, the theatre played an important commercial role in the organisation of people's leisure time.[3] The audience was lured into the many theatres by means of many genres and particularly by means of productions full of images, effects and spectacle.

The same problem occurs in connection with the new points of view and modes of perception presented in this lecture. Besides elements such as sensuous quality, variety, fast pace, there are also negative elements, such as sensationalism and unqualified entertainment and amusement, particularly so since the censorship of the period around 1894 made it virtually impossible to deal with current issues in a critical or satirical vein. The revue was predominantly a genre of the visual *grand spectacle*, intended to kill time. It is equally possible to view what has been described in terms such as "modern modes of perception, visual qualities, pace, stimulation" as precursors of the twentieth-century media, up to and including the Music Video and the Soap Opera, as a superficial form of media terrorism, as empty form, as an example of Neil Postman's "amusing ourselves to death".

The studies about the revue that I am familiar with[4] indicate that there existed, at most, only precursors of the twentieth-century revue in the period around 1894. The shows presented by producers such as Adolph Ernst and Carl Rudolf Cerf and his brother Friedrich in the *Centraltheater* and the *Metropoltheater* make it clear that the ascendancy of the revue only began in 1903 and that its heydays were the days of the Weimar Republic. It is certainly true that the nineteenth century witnessed the early emergence of the revue, but it really flourished between 1903 and 1933, with a break between 1914 and 1918.

I have already said that the lecture given by Christa Hasche provides us with a significant revision of the history of the theatre, because it takes the popular, the trivial theatrical genres as its starting point instead of the more traditional Serious Culture. However, I believe that the lasting paradigmatic revolution was not started by the Revue Theatre, but by the theatre movement, which, after the initiatives taken by naturalists and symbolists, advocated a new dramaturgy, a new scenography, and a need for new ways of acting. Gradually a change came about, initiated from the periphery, which became dominant after 1900 and led to the paradigm of the re-dramatisation, to the autonomy of the dramatic aspects at the cost of the traditionally very strong literary component. By applying a methodological concept such as the 'synchrone Schnitt' of the Reception Theory scholar Hans Robert Jauss, the changes in the year 1894 can be grasped.

Finally, a most important aspect is the fact that later avant-garde producers and directors in various German cultural centres transformed the elements of the popular genres (like the revue) and then successfully used them in their own productions. This applies to *variété*, cabaret, revue, and has to do with the resistance against the literary and verbal theatrical tradition, with the criticism of the illusion of realism and the attempt to develop new visual and gesticulatory forms and to involve the audience more closely. In Munich there were Otto Julius Bierbaum, Oskar Panizza[5] and Wedekind, who used elements of the popular theatre extensively and developed a sensorial form of theatre. In the context of cabaret, we only need to point to the *Elf Scharfrichter* in Munich, and *Schall und Rauch* in Berlin. Such widely divergent producers and directors as Fuchs of the *Münchener Künstlertheater*, Kandinsky, Meyerhold, the Futurists and the Dadaists based themselves on the traditions of the Circus and the *variété*.[6] Piscator profoundly transformed the revue form of the twenties into a theatrical instrument for social criticism[7], in the same way as directors such as Savary, Littlewood and Zadek did after 1945. By rewriting the popular genres, these avant-gardists also tried to undermine these same genres and to use them productively in their own work. Moreover, it was certainly also their intention to save these genres from turning into purely mindless amusement and becoming over-commercialised. To me, this is the main reason why the change in function mentioned by Christa Hasche in the title of her lecture should be connected with the theatrical avant-garde — which, by building on the initiatives taken in the period around 1894, contributed to a new sensibility, to different forms of cultural communication — rather than the development of the revue theatre.

Notes

1. In 1938 Goverts-Verlag published a study by Dolf Sternberger, *Panorama oder Ansichten vom 19. Jahrhundert*. Sternberger's own analysis in *FAZ* of 11 May 1988 is pertinent to this study. In 1980 Stephan Oettermann's monograph *Das Panorama, die Geschichte eines Massamediums* was published (Frankfurt: Syndikat, 1980). In 1985 Cyrille Offermans published his essay 'Bevrijding en verkenning van de blik, het eerste optische massamedium uit de geschiedenis: het panorama,' in: *De mensen zijn mooier dan ze denken* (Amsterdam: De Bezige Bij, 1985). In 1993 the Bundeskunsthalle in Bonn organized a large exhibition around the theme, with a catalogue written by Marie Luise von Plessen.

2. During this symposium on European theatre in and around 1894 various international theatre groups produced plays from this period in the University Theatre in Groningen. Students from Erlangen performed Wedekind's *Die Büchse der Pandora*, for which they had produced extensive and thorough programme notes.

3. Ruth Freydank's book, *Theater in Berlin* (Berlin: Henschel-Verlag, 1988), provides a detailed discussion of these developments.

4. Franz Peter Kothes, *Die theatralische Revue in Berlin und Wien, 1900-1938* (Wilhelmshafen: Heinrichshofen, 1977); Reinhardt Kloos and Thomas Reuter, *Körperbilder, Menschenornamente in Revuetheater und Revuefilm* (Frankfurt: Syndikat, 1980).

5. Cf. Oskar Panizza, 'Der Klassizismus und das Eindringen des Variété. Eine Studie über zeitgenössischen Geschmack,' in: *Die Gesellschaft* (October 1896), pp. 1252-1274.

6. Cf. e.g. the study by Volker Klotz, *Bürgerliches Lachtheater* (Munich: dtv, 1980).

7. Cf. K.J. Hupperetz, 'Berlijn, de revue gepasseerd, aantekeningen bij een theatraal genre,' in: *Akt*, vol. 7 (1983), nr. 3, pp. 49-59.

Rob Erenstein
1894: NEAP TIDE ON THE DUTCH STAGE?

On 1 January 1894 a seemingly despairing critic lamented in *Het Tooneel* (The Stage): "Who will help our theatre back onto its feet? Who will establish a theatre in Amsterdam that is deserving of attention from all who hold the Arts high in their esteem?"[1] He was not alone; two weeks later another critic complained: "It is an apparently seldom occurrence that anything entirely successful is to be found on the Dutch stage."[2]

Besides the complaints, explanations were also attempted. The crisis was the result of a shortage both of original dramatic literature and the lack of vision to foster the development of a loyal audience supporting a stable core of actors.[3] The malaise, however, continued, for in March *Het Tooneel* despondently confirmed that: "The search for innovation (remains) unsuccessful."[4] This handful of complaints can be added to at will. And even the grand celebrations that should have heralded the opening of the new civic theatre on the Leidseplein in Amsterdam were a disappointment: "Of that which should have been an historic moment there remains little worthy of remembering in a month's time."[5]

If the critics are to be believed, 1894 was a year of disasters. Nothing was satisfactory, not even the third tour of Antoine's Théâtre Libre. Moreover, this was boycotted by the critics after the impresario had denied further admittance to Herman Heijermans, who (though a friend of Antoine's), had published a negative review of the first two performances. And the first two visits in 1892 and '93 had been so successful. During these tours people thought they recognized innovation not only in the directing – a concept at that time unknown in the Netherlands – but also in the repertoire and in the acting style – all sadly lacking in anything on offer on Dutch stages.

Despite the accidental nature of its choice, the year 1894 is not without interest for the theatre historian. In retrospect one can determine that this year marked both the end of one line of development and the beginning of a new era. But at the time for those well disposed towards the theatre, the traces of something new were too vague to be recognized as such, so that they only saw the crisis. This feeling was reinforced by the economic crisis that gripped the Netherlands at that time. In 1873 an agricultural crisis had led to a long-term depression that reached its nadir in 1892 and '93. There was a great deal of social unrest, and high unemployment that also affected the theatre. Various theatres and companies went bankrupt and even the famous Salon des Variétés was obliged to close following the sudden death of its director Kreukniet, in spite of desperate attempts by the actors to keep the show going. But even here, it was the end of a phase; from 1894 onwards trade and industry slowly started growing again, while towards the end of the year the SDAP (Sociaal Democratische Arbeiders Partij – the Social Democratic Labour Party) was founded.

Theatre was in a phase of transition throughout Europe, moving from realism to idealism; from *trompe l'oeil* sets that determined the underlying mood to abstract designs that supported ideas and the dramatic content.

Everything was in a state of flux and the pursuit of innovation started from the resistance to the status quo, with Naturalism and, by way of reaction to that, Symbolism, as intermediate stages. Both these trends contributed to change, but their contributions remained limited. The Naturalists' approach was scientific; by collecting characteristic and carefully chosen small facts, they exhibited the human being in his/her continuously changing existence, entirely determined by heredity, surroundings and circumstances. This does not lend itself to the stylized constructions of drama texts and of theatrical performances, limited as they are by time and space.

What was possible in novels did not work on the stage. The result remained limited to a *tranche de vie*, a slice of life. As Aristotle already understood so well, theatre concentrates on inner growth taking place within conflict situations, so that both the characters and the audience gain insights into the essence of existence. A work such as *Thérèse Raquin* by the champion of Naturalists, Emile Zola, was limited to melodramatic scenes, far removed from the cool analysis required by theory. The importance of Antoine as a theatre innovator and of his Théâtre Libre lies in the new style of acting, his attention to ensemble acting, and the creation of the fourth wall, which earned him admiration in the Netherlands. The impact made by his repertoire was less pronounced, though the crude scenes depicting the daily life of the people staged alongside more usual works — he was obliged, after all, to work without subsidies and had to consider his income — illicited some shocked responses.[6]

In reaction to Antoine's material realism, Symbolism turned away from the visible world and directed itself to the being behind the façade. External form symbolized an elusive essence. Through his Théâtre de l'Oeuvre, Lugné-Poe tried to give shape to these ideas on the stage, the suggestive power of Maeterlinck's works being among the few that rendered themselves amenable to this task. Lugné-Poe soon recognized the need to widen his repertoire with non-Symbolist works, but tried to develop an anti-naturalistic style of acting and direction that consisted of a somewhat monotone declamation with a minimum of external action. He was a good actor and a sensitive director who allowed his actors space to interpret their own roles, while maintaining the unity of the ensemble through a well-managed discipline. During his guest performances in the Netherlands he impressed especially by his acting and the unity of the whole. Nonetheless, the critics were reserved and, on the occasion of his tour of the Netherlands in 1895, suggested, for example, that the quality of the acting was essentially indistinguishable from that of any other travelling French company.

Finally, Ibsen's great contribution to innovation should not go unmentioned. His attack on the closed world-view that theatre performances had until that time shown their audiences was one of the most important contributions to innovation, but could only succeed completely when an appropriate acting style had been developed in which the ensemble took centre stage. Nor is it surprising that both Antoine and Lugné-Poe took his work into their repertoires. The social unrest prevailing in Europe was given expression in the social drama written by French (Becque, Brieux) as well as German authors, the undisputed champion among whom was Hauptmann, whose *Die Weber* achieved a *succès fou* in Paris. In the Netherlands it was Herman Heijermans who would pursue this course with success.

But of these many innovations, little was noticeable among the Dutch companies. At the time, theatre was still a pastime for well-to-do citizens expecting to be entertained: something enjoyable to aid digestion after a good dinner. One went to the civic theatre in Amsterdam to see *Madame sans Gêne* or *Gismonda*. And the piece most frequently performed in the civic theatre in 1895 was Feydeau's *Hôtel de Libre Échange* (Hotel Paradiso) which was performed no less than twenty times. The most frequently performed original Dutch-language production was Vondel's *Gijsbreght* which totalled five performances.

Theatre is a social art form that gives the spectator a mirror-image of his own age. What the audience were shown in the mirror in 1894 was scarcely uplifting and is best defined as being respectable, bourgeois and having a distinguished air of gentility. It was a theatre of lethargic complacency, as can be gleaned, among other things, from the reaction to innovations abroad: one registered their occurrence with little enthusiasm. In neighbouring countries, Ibsen's work, for example, was the source of many a theatre scandal and led to vehement polemics pivoting on whether his work should be permitted in public theatres. *Ghosts* — described in *Het Tooneel* as "clever and loathsome" — was adopted by many innovative companies abroad in protest at the prevalent theatre traditions and as a sort of manifesto. The subsequent scandal was always good advertising.

This was not the case in the Netherlands where Ibsen, following a less than successful *Pillars of Society* in 1880, was performed regularly from 1889 onwards without ever leading to any form of breach of the peace. The appearance of his works was registered with a certain amount of shock after which everything returned to routine. Reviewers treated Ibsen's characters like cases of a disease they would happily never experience in their daily lives. Characters displayed in circumstances so unlikely, it was hardly worth wasting many words on them. And yet the quality was recognized and already in the 1890s *A Doll's House* was hailed as a classic, from which the audience could derive the lesson that in a good marriage one should avoid an Ibsenesque situation by not keeping too many secrets from each other.

The didactic value of a play was an important criterion in its assessment and that explains why the most popular of Ibsen's plays in the Netherlands, *Hedda Gabler*, was given a negative evaluation in the 1890s. This thoroughly "morbid, sickly and inartistic woman" was driven by unprecedentedly destructive impulses, or so it was thought, and was written off as the ultimate form of theatrical meaninglessness, because her nihilism rendered the derivation of any moral values impossible. Hedda was dubbed a *canaille* suffering from a *fin-de-siècle* neurosis and petty bourgeois shallowness. She was consumed with unsatiated animal passions and the too high price of pleasure filled her with cowardly fear.[7] And despite this harsh judgement, the play was performed time and again!

For Strindberg's *The Father* there was even less understanding among the critics. Some critics found the content so indecent that they refused to summarize it. One critic proposed "that one would have to be half a psychiatrist to form a correct opinion on it....This play fails to exalt, to teach, or to warn." Note here the three criteria with which a good play should comply.

In the case of Ibsen and Strindberg it had much to do with their status as modernists, but the phlegmatic Dutch audiences also closed their eyes to the highest quality of traditional theatre as well. When Eleonora Duse's unique talent could be admired in this country in 1895 as many as one in five of the performances of *La Dame aux Camélias* had to be cancelled due to lack of interest, while the remaining four were only moderately attended. Tickets to performances by the actress who had the whole of Europe at her feet were considered too highly priced for the sober Dutchman: seven guilders and fifty cents plus five per cent tax. That was certainly high, and what did one get in return? The critics, some of whom were initially sceptical in the face of Duse's much trumpeted arrival, were electrified by her acting and were unanimous in their judgements: the "highest achievement" in the art. The seamlessness of the character caused one critic to be overcome with the fear that it was not Marguerite Gautier but Duse herself who was dying. *Het Handelsblad* noted: "Whoever is guilty of absenting himself is not worthy ever to take pleasure from art again." And in the survey of the 1894-'95 season *Het Tooneel* wrote: "The performances of Eleonora Duse stood out beyond any other. A theatre season is rescued if just one of her performances can be enjoyed; she gave four, which were, however, poorly attended."

The Dutch audiences had their own theatrical stars, epitomizing a middle-class taste with clear distinctions from that of the rest of Europe. If France could lay claim to great stars such as Sarah Bernhardt, Coquelin and Mrs. Ségond-Wéber, in Germany actors such as Kainz and Mitterwurzer were the heavenly bodies of the great classics, and in England Ellen Terry and Henry Irving were a unique pair of considerable allure. Italy possessed the greatest of them all in Eleonora Duse. However, in the Netherlands Mrs Kleine-Gartman (1818-1885) — nicknamed Mietje Kleine — and L.J. Veltman (1817-1907) were the most popular and even more famous than Louis Bouwmeester. In contrast to their famous foreign colleagues, they lacked the allure of stars, nor were they great tragic actors. Mrs Kleine-Gartman was carried aloft by her Amsterdam audiences and took her leave of the stage with one of her greatest successes: the title role in Schimmel's *Jufvrouw Serklaes* (Mistress Serklaes), in which she played "a more cunning than sagacious middle-class woman in the midst of the gentility of the court of Brussels". After her death in 1885 her memory lived on. At the opening of the new civic theatre in

Amsterdam in 1894, a short play composed by Schimmel for the occasion as part of the *spectacle coupé* was performed in which the author summarized once again his by that time outdated artistic credos. A play is not so important, he stated, but rather what the actors could do with it and he recollected how Mietje Kleine had been wont to say: "It is not so much a question of *drawing it out*, as of *putting it in*."

And Veltman, the kindly Veltman, was famous in particular as the villain, not in tragic roles, but in mere traitors' parts he could cast a spell over a large audience. He was an inadequate speaker of verse, a simple man and yet an artist among thousands. "The average middle-class man was primarily Veltman's admirer and probably the average middle-class woman even more so."

The preference of Dutch audiences for precisely such stage heroes in contrast to the virtuoso stars favoured by foreign audiences makes it quite clear that Dutch theatre culture had a character entirely of its own. Performances of the foreign repertoire presented here — and in our 'loan culture' that was about 95 per cent — were adjusted to conform to this middle-class character. It was not the grand gesture that counted, but rather natural acting based on realism. To be carried away by grand passions was not what the audience wanted, rather to empathize affectionately with the main characters.

In this way, Dutch theatre pursued its own course of development until by 1894 it seemed to have reached a deadlock. This seems to be a sad conclusion, but it can be construed from a positive perspective as the successful outcome of the proposed aims of the seventies to elevate Dutch theatre, of which the opening of the new civic theatre in Amsterdam on 1 September 1894 formed the climax.

Around 1870 the struggle had begun to raise theatre in the Netherlands to a higher plane, and to drive away the spectators with caps on their heads and a wad of tobacco in their mouths who peopled the civic theatre in favour of the respectable middle-classes. And what actually happened?

The theatre that at the beginning of the 19th century had been compared favourably with the best in Europe had become stranded because of the aloofness of the government. By viewing the civic theatre as merely a profitable venture for exploitation, and by refusing to make a contribution to culture, the civic theatre in Amsterdam, for example, was repeatedly let to the highest bidder. This encouraged a pandering to the taste of the masses and the avoidance of every artistic risk. In this way, not only did all signs of refinement vanish from the acting and the repertoire, but educated audiences also disappeared from the civic theatre, to be replaced by increasingly simple people demanding melodramas and dancing routines, and applauding actors from their own ranks who, with powerful voices and strong Amsterdam accents, could give their best to foreign melodramas such as *Ben Leil of de zoon van den Nacht* (Ben Leil, or the Son of the Night) or *Abellino of de groote bandiet* (Abellino, or the Great Bandit) in handsomely fashioned stock sets, preferably with plenty of spectacle.

Performances of this type inspired J.A. Alberdingk Thijm, in the *Spectator van Tooneel* (Theatre Spectator, 1842-'50), to the most vicious of criticism out of sorrow and anger at the decay of the theatre. He spoke of a "steaming pool of mud" and of a "reservoir of the filthiest hogwash of outlandish literatures". Neither would Amsterdam's magistrates be spared his bile, because they were only interested in making money from the civic theatre instead of giving it a subsidy. And when in 1849 a variety-show director from the Nes, De Vries by name, was favoured with the license to the civic theatre, Thijm wrote in his *Spectator*: "Gentlemen of the executive council of the far-famed city of Amsterdam! We wanted to be Emperor of all the Asiatic-Japanese empire — we recommend to you all the simple hari kiri!"

It was only around 1870 that this period of indifference with regard to culture and the policies of the civic theatre by citizens and administration came to a close. This was as a result of civic interference in the arts; though rather from the need by citizens to advance the interests of their own class than from idealistic considerations.[8] This led to the foundation of "Het Nederlandsch Tooneelverbond" (The Dutch Theatre Union) in 1870, that still had to work without government subsidy. Its aim was to get the national theatre out of its blind alley by improving the actors and the repertoire.

With few exceptions, the actors opted to sit on the fence and wait, which is hardly surprising because a precondition for change was a relationship of trust between the closed circle of the theatre world and the well-intentioned, critical outsiders. As a first step on the new road a periodical was published, *Het Nederlandsch Tooneel* (after 1882 in brief *Het Tooneel*), that from October 1871 would attempt to improve standards in general by criticism of performances, actors and other related matters.

The next step was to found a drama school, which was set up in 1874 after a great deal of discussion. It was here that prospective actors would be prepared, not only technically, but also through a planned general education with a view to emphasising the arts. Finally, in 1875 there followed the establishment of the Vereeniging "Het Nederlandsch Tooneel" (The Association "The Dutch Theatre"), to which in the following year the civic theatres of The Hague and Amsterdam were assigned.

But these innovations by no means settled matters. They were introduced with difficulty, because the actors as well as their audiences and critics had to be won over to the new theatre. The inspirational leader of this movement was H.J. Schimmel, a late Romantic author and successful playwright who, as the most important member of the Board of Directors, determined artistic policy.

Schimmel did not hold the audiences in high esteem, so he chose a slow and steady pace by which to educate them. He started with plays by Scribe and Sardou alternated every now and again with spectacular pieces or fairytale ballets. In his estimation the time was not yet ripe for Shakespeare, and he paid a great deal of attention to historically accurate costumes, responsive acting, diction and cutting back on the time-honoured use of pathos.

In those early years, renewal was certainly far from easy, because the first wave from the drama school had still not graduated and the old guard would hardly allow itself to be transformed overnight, and, they were of the opinion, moreover, that the school of the fairground theatre itself was the only place where youthful talent could unfold itself. Schimmel's passionate hopes for a blossoming of dramatic literature also failed to come about to begin with.

The results were so disappointing that in 1879 the licence to play in the civic theatre was not extended and Het Nederlandsch Tooneel was obliged to proceed elsewhere in a trimmed down version of itself. At the time the company had the opportunity to work with predominantly young actors from the theatre school to shape them into a unified whole, while the arrival of Bouwmeester, a natural talent from the fairground, proved a noteworthy reinforcement. In 1882 the company returned to the civic theatre with a subsidy from the monarch and received the designation "royal".

They continued to stage their performances with varying success, but the actors themselves were increasingly dissatisfied with Schimmel's policies, with his choice of repertoire, with the strict hierarchy and with the old-fashioned system of casting roles that he rigidly adhered to as he effectively gagged the directors and actors themselves. In 1889 everything came to a head, when the young actors and Rössing, the secretary of the Board of Directors, resigned. Subsequently he founded the *Tooneelvereeniging* (Theatre Association). An escalation of hostilities was pre-empted, however, on 20th February 1890, when the civic theatre on the Leidseplein burned to the ground.

The burnt-out civic theatre offered the Board of Directors a unique chance to leap into the future by replacing it with a modern theatre building. However, quite the reverse came about. The innovators of 1876 built the theatre of their dreams, which was, however, dated by 1894. The new theatre was planned as a prestigious symbol with the allure of eminence: "The auditorium gives the impression of gentility and conscious wealth. Whoever sits there knows that he sits there; he sees himself and can feel that others see him. If he were going there to a wedding ceremony, he would not be admitted without formal attire. This is what he feels."[9]

The concept of a civic theatre as a people's theatre was definitively laid to rest and Leo Simons' plea directly after the fire for a civic theatre of the people without the distinctions of where one sits and how much one pays as in the concert hall found no response. Class distinctions were firmly underlined in the structure; whereas the privileged audience members followed a broad marble staircase to the auditorium and balconies, the cheap seats were only approachable from a separate entrance and narrow stone stairs to the galleries strictly divorced from the rest of the building with their own foyer. And this situation exists to this day!

The whole building, Neo-Renaissance in style, was the jewel in the crown of the previous era, a status symbol without a vision of the future. The criticism was hardly positive: "Due to one's continual tripping over the details from which the whole is comprised, it is very difficult to form an opinion."[10]
Theatre should be uplifting and the somber works following modern trends, those by the naturalists and Ibsen (whose talent he recognized) should be avoided. With this Schimmel took a disappointed and slightly bitter leave of the Koninklijke Vereeniging that was consolidating the crisis in its very policies while victory was being celebrated: the people had been driven from the civic theatre and the respectable middle-classes took their places in the new building.
By these criteria 1894 was a successful year, and to give credit where it is due, Rössing, who had left the Koninklijke Vereeniging in anger in 1889, was right when he remarked on the departure of Schimmel: "Schimmel was the one who elevated the social position of the actor and brought repute to the stage."[11]
Happily there was more theatre being made than that to be had in the Amsterdam civic theatre, where citizens of standing were feasting themselves and only those plays were performed that had already proven their worth abroad.

At all times and in all places artists can be found who test the boundaries of established tradition — even in the Dutch theatre of those days and in spite of the crisis that elicited so many complaints. And in this way a new era was gradually introduced through small more or less successful experiments. An inventory of what was achieved in 1894 is not as disappointing as might be expected. Innovation came about from a combination of something specifically Dutch with the influences from foreign trends.
A characteristic of Dutch theatre was — and still is — a certain aversion to grand gestures and pomp and circumstance. Even in royal characters the Dutch would rather recognize something of their own bourgeois mentality. It was this tendency that enabled Mrs Kleine-Gartman to become the most popular actress of her time. The power of her performance lay in simplicity without pathos. Through this objective approach to her roles she made herself convincing and touched the sober hearts of the Dutch spectators, who would always be inclined to remark along with Multatuli's Droogstoppel: "And still more lies on the stage. When the hero exits with his stiff comic steps to save the fatherland, why do the double doors at the back always open of their own accord?"
It is hardly surprising that from this sobriety Rotterdam, the port and trading city, would develop a straightforward and sober acting style in the 70s that would find appreciation among the general public. And to such an extent that in 1879, after three disappointing early years of the Vereeniging "Het Nederlandsch Tooneel", the civic theatre on the Leidseplein was granted to the Rotterdammers, who, also after three difficult years of playing both

venues at the same time, would be obliged by their huge budget deficit to retreat to their Rotterdam base.

This natural and sober acting – partly stimulated by the abolition of the old-fashioned system of casting roles in 1874 – showed itself in its best light in plays depicting simple folk in their own environments such as those in the works of Rosier Faassen whose dramatic oeuvre numbers more than twenty plays, including box-office successes like *Anne-Mie*, *De Ledige Wieg* (The Vacant Crib) and the one-act play *Manus de Snorder* (Manus the Coachman). With regard to this style of acting Hunningher has claimed: "This cannot be connected with realism as an artistic trend, but when that trend infiltrated our country it found its bed already made up for it, while in Amsterdam the necessary obstacles had first to be cleared away."[12]

The Koninklijke Vereeniging, under Schimmel's strict leadership, retained its system of casting roles and a repertoire of plays in romantic tone and magnificent settings that had proved themselves abroad. It was not from the Leidseplein that innovation would come along, but rather from a young generation of theatre-makers who established the Tooneelvereeniging as a protest against Schimmel's choice of repertoire and inspired by developments abroad. It was their aim to give a single model performance along the lines of the new insights, using actors borrowed from a number of companies. They chose Ibsen's *A Doll's House* and Molière's *Les Précieuses Ridicules*. The two performances they gave on 28 March and 9 April 1889 were both successful and influential. A tour of the country followed and in the subsequent season the initiative was pursued by the company of Kreukniet and Poolman in the Salon des Variétés, because they could see in the new repertoire sufficient return on their investment.

A special subscribers' series of the modern repertoire was performed alongside the usual popular box-office attractions such as *De Twee Weezen* (The Two Orphans) and *Marmeren Beelden - IJskoude Harten* (Marble Statues - Ice-Cold Hearts). Here, in this new repertoire and modern acting style young performers and spectators could come into contact with each other. The term 'modern' acting should be interpreted by us, according to the critics at that time, as down-to-earth acting.[13]

The Koninklijke Vereeniging had no intention of being left behind in the competition and produced Ibsen's *Wild Duck*. However, as result of the strict system of casting roles and a concomitant lack of experience with ensemble acting, this performance remained noticeably below the standard of the Salon des Variétés. And this led once again to criticism of Schimmel's artistic policies. The fire in the civic theatre on 20 February 1890 put a temporary end to the competition, while the economic crisis and the death of Kreukniet in the spring of 1893 levelled the Salon des Variétés. Not for long, however; in the autumn the Nederlandsche Tooneelvereeniging opened its doors under the leadership of Louis Chrispijn Sr. Actually, even this was a result of the prevalent economic crisis which also impeded the companies from keeping the students from the drama school under contract or even from taking them on. And now this new trained generation combined under Chrispijn, at first in the Paleis van Volksvlijt, and then from January 1894 onwards to perform throughout the winter season in the Salon des Variétés, while travelling around the fairs in the spring and summer in order to survive financially.

Their initiative was too small-scale and their success too disputed for them to be recognized by the critics as the ray of hope in the dark year of 1894. Furthermore, the critics also failed to recognize that the initiative by the Tooneelvereeniging in 1889 would inspire Dutch writers to pick up their pens. Where the generation of the 80s failed, because as *l'art pour l'art* artists they were too involved with their own emotions, the next generation would succeed. And in the Salon des Variétés they found both Kreukniet and Chrispijn willing to provide a podium for their work. Heijermans made his debut in 1893 with *Dora Kremer* which flopped, but he triumphed two months later with a piece written under a pseudonym, *Ahasverus*, which would be successfully staged by Antoine in Paris in the same year. His later work would also be produced by the Nederlandsche Tooneelvereeniging.

In Rotterdam, Kreukniet's example was followed by Jan C. de Vos, who in 1890-95 performed in the Tivolitheater where the work of many Dutch authors was produced. Nouhuys made his debut in the Tivoli in 1890 with his much produced *Eerloos* (Infamy), along with modern foreign works. Sadly the audiences were small and this compelled him to re-introduce farces and melodramas to flesh out their income. Because he was obliged to tour a great deal in order to make ends meet, he had, in particular, considerable influence in the provinces.

The new Dutch repertoire that came into existence during those years did not fit seamlessly with the large-scale foreign trends, but was characterized in particular by a type of Dutch 'living room' realism, with much attention to fine detail, which was so recognizable that it reaped success. Especially when more authors started to acquire the ability to write plays. Due to the Rotterdam origins of this realism, in 1925 Leo Simons could demonstrate that of thirty-five playwrights who made their debut since 1890, ninety per cent originated from Rotterdam!

Although the total number of original Dutch works initially on offer was merely five per cent of the total, after 1890 this steadily increased to approximately twenty per cent in the early decades of the twentieth century, a situation not known since the seventeenth century. The Nederlandsche Tooneelvereeniging took a large measure of the credit for this, for in 1908, on the occasion of their fifteenth anniversary, no less than *seventy* of their 156 productions were originally Dutch.

This could not have been foreseen by the pessimists in 1894, of whom one concluded that: "Here at home the theatre companies play to empty houses when they perform a piece that transcends the usual standards and play to full houses a week long with monstrosities drawn from the old box of spectacular pieces such as *Gier-Wally*, *Keraban de Stijfhoofdige* (Keraban the Blockhead) and *De Graaf van Lavernie* (The Count of Lavernie)."[14]

As I have already pointed out, it was an age of social unrest. There were many strikes, the SDAP was founded and many of the new generation of playwrights expressed a personal ethos that bore some affinity with the new social movements. Heijermans' membership of the SDAP, which he joined in 1895, was an obvious example of this. His plays remained largely taboo in the Leidseplein theatre where the norm was steadfast: "respectable, bourgeois and gentile." This demonstrates that the struggle on the stage between the old and the new was equally a reflection of the social struggle for progress. In any case the struggle for theatrical innovations began in 1894 and this was partly due to the innovators of the seventies who endeavoured, among other things, to train emancipated and self-aware actors who would be socially acceptable rather than the outcasts they had been taken for. In this purpose they were also successful. In 1895 Henri Dekking noted: "Nowadays one can be the open friend of theatre people without compromising oneself."[15]

Neap tide does not exist in history, which is constantly in movement and development. But these movements are sometimes difficult to perceive when you are yourself a part of that process. In Dutch theatre history 1894 was just such a moment.

Notes

1. *Het Tooneel* (The Stage), XXIII, no. 7, 1 January 1894, p. 43.

2. *Idem*, XXIII, no. 8, 15 January 1894, p. 46.

3. *Idem*, p. 54.

4. *Idem*, XXIII, no. 11, 1 March 1894, p. 66.

5. *Idem*, XXIV, no. 1, 1 October 1894, p. 5.

6. The subjects chosen by a new generation of authors become the cause of much debate. The public is at a loss and opinions are actually twofold. As has been supposed, the modern movement chooses to show life as it is. Artists take models that in reality one would rather shy away from. But the most modern artists went even further and show the public venal women and drunken women. How should a critic react to this? The answer is: it is not so much the processed idea that the critic has to judge (without doubt whatever he shows will exist in reality), but rather the way the idea is placed before him. If, moreover, all the misery in Sudermann's *Vlinders* (Butterflies) actually exists (and why should it not?), is it right for this to be shown by means of a performance and offered as food for thought.
The author who takes all this into consideration ends his argument with: "In brief: to me a drunken woman is one of the worst things there is, but Yvette Gilbert's *La Soularde* is something I would rather not miss." *Het Tooneel*, XXV, no. 3, p. 14.

7. *Het Tooneel*, XX, no. 12, p. 92.

8. E. Boekman, *Overheid en kunst in Nederland* (Government and the Arts in The Netherlands) (Amsterdam, 1939), p. 68.

9. J.H. Rössing, quoted by H.H.J. de Leeuwe, 'De geschiedenis van het Amsterdamsche tooneel in de negentiende eeuw (1795-1925)' (The History of Amsterdam Theatre in the 19th Century [1795-1925]), in: A.E. d'Ailly (ed.), *Zeven eeuwen Amsterdam* (Seven centuries of Amsterdam). Amsterdam: Scheltema and Holkema (6 volumes), vol. V, pp. 113-55, esp. p. 136.

10. Quoted from *Architectura* in *Het Tooneel*, XXIV, no. 1, 1 October 1894, p. 6.

11. Quoted by B. Hunningher, *Een eeuw Nederlands Tooneel* (A Century of Dutch Theatre), (Amsterdam: Querido, 1949), p. 71.

12. B. Hunningher, *Toneel en Werkelijkheid* (Stage and Reality), (Rotterdam: Brusse, 1947), p. 22.

13. *Het Tooneel*, XXIII, no. 2, 15 October, 1893, p. 14. The acting of Louis Bouwmeester in a particular performance is referred to here as "distinguished and modern". The critic added in the same breath: "And in modernity I admire particularly sobriety."

14. See note 1.

15. Henri M. Dekking, *Het Leven van Willem van Zuylen* (The Life of Willem van Zuylen, as related by himself and retold by), Amsterdam 1895, p. 1. Concerning the social position of the Dutch actor in the 19th century see also: R.L. Erenstein, 'De Emancipatie van de Acteur in de Negentiende Eeuw' (The Emancipation of the Actor in the 19th Century). In: *Tijdschrift voor Geschiedenis*, 104, nr. 3 (1991), pp. 381-95.

Mary Kemperink
1894: BREAKTHROUGH OF THE MODERN THEATRE IN THE NETHERLANDS[1]

In the preceding article by Rob Erenstein the situation in which the Dutch theatre found itself in the year 1894, is epitomised as an artistic crisis, a crisis however with some rays of hope for the future.

In reaction to this vision, I would like to pursue the following two aspects. Firstly, the qualification of 1894 as a crisis and the suggestion in this regard that Dutch theatre was lagging behind developments abroad.

Secondly, the qualification of Naturalism as a literary movement unfit to express itself by means of drama.

As for the first aspect, let me give some facts. As from 1880, after Meiningen's first visit to our country in the same year, classical theatre was shown here on stage. I name Shakespeare's *Romeo and Juliet* (1879), *Othello* (1880), *Hamlet* (1882), *Richard III* (1884), *Macbeth* (1887), *A Winter's Tale* (1887) and *The Merchant of Venice* (1880 and 1892). These new performances were quite successful. For the Dutch public, the famous actor Louis Bouwmeester was since then closely linked to his role of Shylock in *The Merchant of Venice*.

More important in this respect was the attention paid to the realistic-naturalistic part of the repertory. In 1879, Ibsen's *The pillars of society* had been far from a success. In 1889, however, his *Nora* (*A Doll's House*) was performed twenty five times. The play was put forthwith on the programme of two different theatre groups in the subsequent year. His *Ghosts, The Wild Duck* and *Hedda Gabler* followed soon thereafter.

During the visits of the French theatre-maker André Antoine to our country in 1892 and 1893, most of the critics were struck with admiration by the natural way in which he made his actors perform on stage. The critics were also full of admiration for the original new plays he brought, such as *Blanchette* by Eugène Brieux and *La fille Elisa*, based on a novel by Edmond de Goncourt. Within a year, *Blanchette* was put on the programme by two theatre companies at the same time. As of 1890 we see that serious and well esteemed Dutch writers such as Marcellus Emants and Van Nouhuys, strong defenders of the naturalistic novel, now tried to create something comparable in theatre, thus competing with Ibsen and Brieux. Just as De Goncourt's *La fille Elisa*, Louis Couperus' novel *Footsteps of Fate* was adapted for stage. According to the critics, it was a play that could stand comparison with French and Scandinavian naturalists.

New theatre groups with an Antoine-like signature were founded; such as the Tooneelvereeniging (founded in 1889), the company of De Vos & Korelaar (founded in 1890) and the group of Kreukniet & Poolman (founded in 1890), which after Kreukniet's death in 1893 was more or less taken over by Louis Chrispijn (founded in 1893).

All these facts together justify in my opinion the conclusion that a new, more authentic, realistic way of writing and acting took over from so called well-made plays and public-conscious performances. In the criticism of the early nineties one finds qualifications as: the play has been 'lived' rather then 'acted'. And actors such as Louis Chrispijn and Jan de Vos were considered to be the two Dutch Antoine's, just as earlier the famous actress Theo Bouwmeester had time and again been named the Dutch Sarah Bernhardt. This shows not only a mere dependence on foreign developments but, also a great interest and admiration for the latest developments on the stage in Berlin, London and above all in Paris. The disappointment over Antoine's last visit to our country in 1894 should in my view not be seen as a sign of hostility or distaste with respect to the new naturalistic movement in France. Quite to the contrary, this disappointment was merely a sign of disapproval: disapproval of the loss of quality Antoine's players showed that very year. By then, many of his gifted actors had left and his tour was organized in such a hurry that indeed no great results could be expected. Antoine later admitted his failure in a private interview with Herman Heijermans. The disapproval of Antoine's tour, which was shown by the critics, paved the way for a new theatrical interpretation, whereby the play was to be considered as a slice of life rather than a moralistic fairy tale.

To a lesser extent than Rob Erenstein I tend to describe the year 1894 as bourgeois or out of date. The reason for this is not only a question of accents. The main reason is the fact that in such an qualification no distinction is made between the audience on the one hand and the critics, theatre-makers and actors on the other hand. In my view, this distinction is vital to get a clear understanding of the Dutch theatre in 1894.

During most of the 19th century the so called upper middle classes showed some disdain for the Dutch theatre. Perhaps it was the influence of French culture or some inferiority complex with which our nation is affected, that made people consider things from abroad much more worthwhile than their national artistic products. This attitude together with the economic decline in our country made that the theatres tried in the first place to maximise turnover, rather than aiming at realising quality plays for a small public. Consequently, theatres, filled with a lower middle class audience asking for melodrama and farce, prospered.

After 1880 however, we see that a new public is won for Dutch theatre. A public with a distinct taste for literature that is willing to consider theatre as an art. It is a small public, however, formed mainly by young intellectuals and artists, who despise the bad and old-fashioned taste of the masses. It is against this bad taste that the critics protest. Their comments show that standards have changed in a few years time; they should not be considered as evidence for the decline of the Dutch theatre.

Frankly speaking, our country did not differ at all from other countries. It should be borne in mind that in the same year the leading theatres in Paris at the *rive droite* still derived their celebrity from drawing room plays and vaudevilles. Secondly, one should not forget that the avant-garde plays of Antoine were performed in Paris for a much smaller audience than in

Holland. It is significant in this respect to learn that Antoine was able to clear his debts from the proceeds of his tours in Holland and Belgium.

Now I come to my second issue: the qualification of the naturalistic theatre in general as a paradox. The key-point in this respect is the postulate that the influence of race and environment can not be demonstrated by means of a play. In my view this conclusion is less accurate in two aspects.

Firstly, looking at the development of the novel in relation to naturalism, we see that it necessarily tends to incorporate aspects of drama. The narratological structure tends to be substituted by dramatic patterns: the scenic presentation is put in the foreground to the detriment of the narrator. A Dutch novelist characterised this phenomenon as: 'the writer hidden between the wings'. Provided the rules of objective representation are carefully and consequently observed, this leads to a novel that differs only one step from a play, as is shown in the novel *Papa Hamlet* by the German writers Schlaf and Holz.

Secondly, in my opinion and that of others, naturalism in theatre as well as in the novel is much more than just a demonstration of the positivist determination by race and environment. Naturalist plays as well as naturalist novels have many other characteristics. Determinism is only one of them. Such other characteristics are: a lack of intrigue, a natural dialogue, themes related to modern life and the absence of a happy end. A confirmation of this is not only to be found in the plays itself but also in the theories of Zola, Antoine, Holz, Schlaf and Strindberg.

Thus, naturalism may be characterised as a fruitful formula, that has given birth to a refreshingly new form of theatre, both from the viewpoint of the play as of the acting. In respect of the plays, I would not support the remark that these are contrary to the Aristotelian formula. It is no coincidence that contemporary critics of Zola, Brieux and Ibsen compared their works to classical tragedy. Just like Oedipus the naturalist protagonists struggle in vain against blind fate.

Note

1. This short article treats in a nutshell an episode of the Dutch theatre which has been elaborated by the same author in her study *Nederlands toneel in het fin de siècle (1890-1900)* (Amsterdam: AUP, 1995).

Ivo Kuyl
THE OBJECTIVITY OF PARODY.
OBSERVATIONS ON CHEKHOV'S LITERARY AESTHETICS

Introduction

In her lecture Herta Schmid* focused on Stanislavsky's directorial views. She pointed out how his views are rooted in three schools of 19th century theatre: Pushkin's romantic school, Gogol and Sochovo-Kobylin's school of realism and Ostrovski's socially critical realism.

This presentation could easily lead to the notion that Chekhov's work is also rooted in the same tradition. It is after all still quite common to regard Chekhov in terms of Stanislavsky's naturalistic notions about theatre. This is quite understandable, if we bear in mind that the performances of the Moscow Art Theatre, headed by Stanislavsky and Nemirovic-Danchenko, not only rehabilitated Chekhov as a playwright, but also gave him a place in the world repertory.

Nevertheless I believe there are reasons to question the naturalistic nature of Chekhov's work. I intend to show that his literary aesthetics are irreconcilable with the notions about art held in realism and naturalism.

I will start out by elaborating on Chekhov's epistemological ideas. Secondly I will show how these ideas form the basis of the objective method Chekhov applies in his plays. I hope to clarify that 'objectivity' in Chekhov is quite something else than 'objectivity' in the context of realism/naturalism. Thirdly I will claim that Chekhov's work is fundamentally parodical and pay closer attention to an interesting, intertextual form of parody, described by Vera Gottlieb in *Chekhov and the Vaudeville.*[1] In the final section of this paper I will discuss three major differences between realism and naturalism on the one hand and Chekhov's literary aesthetics on the other hand.

Chekhov's epistemological views

One of the reasons why Chekhov's work seems so modern and contemporary is his scepticism concerning the nature of knowledge. From a philosophical perspective Chekhovs epistemological position is characterized by an overall mistrust of traditional metaphysics in which opposing terms such as truth and lie, good and evil, beauty and ugliness are mutually exclusive.

In Chekhov, however, these polar opposites seem to flow into one and appear to be joined in extreme ambivalence. The following quote was passed down by Alexander Kuprin, a contemporary of Chekhov, and illustrates the above:

> In life, there are no clear-cut consequences or reasons; in it, everything is mixed up together; the important and the paltry, the great and the

base, the tragic and the ridiculous. One is hypnotized and enslaved by routine and cannot manage to break away from it. What are needed are new forms, new ones.[2]

One might call Chekhov, like Hegel, a "dialectical" thinker, seeing that he defends the unity of oppositions against the dualism of metaphysics. Still, there is a fundamental difference between the two. Hegel states that thesis and antithesis are continually resolved in a higher synthesis, until the closed system of abstract notions is reached in which being and thinking pervade each other completely.[3]

Chekhov's dialectic, however, does not culminate in any higher truth. He acknowledges the existence of a deep and insurpassable gap between being and thinking. Reality always retains some of its mystery and incomprehensibility. Chekhov agrees with Voltaire and Socrates, who realized that "we indeed cannot understand anything at all in this world". He would consider it "a major spiritual enrichment and a great step forward" if only "the artist would come round to admitting that he understands nothing about what he sees."[4]

The nature of Chekhov's objectivity

As the quotation passed down by Kuprin illustrates, Chekhov's quest for new theatrical forms was inspired greatly by his insight into the dialectical structure of reality. Chekhov rejects the idea that literature is a mere vehicle, a neutral form designed to communicate a message or moral lesson represented by "heroes" or "villains". He also rejects the artificial distinction between tragedy and comedy. Both the tragic and the comic are simultaneously present in Chekhov's work.

Perhaps the best way to gain insight into the innovative quality of Chekhov's work is to try to discover what he meant exactly when he stated that any literary writer should be *objective*. If we take a closer look at this term, it appears that what Chekhov considered it to be had little to do with what it means in realism or naturalism.

To begin with, one should bear in mind that Chekhov thought every creative process should start out with a question:

> That no questions and only answers exist within his scope [that of the artist], will only be stated by one who has never himself written any literature and who has never created images. The artist observes, chooses, guesses, combines. These very actions presuppose a question. If he had not asked himself a question at the onset there would have been nothing to guess or choose.[6]

But what kind of questions are we concerned with here? They are not scientific or philosophical questions, or questions dealing with technical or practical matters:

> In conversations with my fellows in art I always maintain that it is not the artist's task to solve specific questions. It is not right for an artist to concern himself with what he does not understand. For specific subjects we have specialists. It is up to them to pass judgment on the agricultural community, the changeability of capital, the drawbacks of drunkenness, the pros and cons of wearing boots, women's diseases... The artist should only judge what he understands. His view is as limited as that of any specialist. This is what I repeat and maintain at all times.[7]

According to Chekhov the writer should not come up with any new theories concerning questions such as "What is a solar eclipse?" "What is morally right?" or "How could I diminish unemployment with 25,000 units within two years?" Nor should he concern himself with whether any existing theory is true or false, whether it is good or bad. These matters are beyond the scope of men of letters. They are for all kinds of specialists, such as physicists, moral philosophers, economists, etcetera.
The literary writer has his own specialisation. First and foremost he treats the phenomena he portrays as constructs, as interpretations of mankind or as human artifacts. Moreover he makes no attempt to explain a phenomenon as a moment in the teleological development of the mind (as Hegel would do for instance), or as a phase in the progressive and necessary development towards truth. It does, however, seem that the writer has to ask questions concerning the nature and function of a phenomenon:

> You wrote that the conversation about pessimism nor Kisoschka's story further the matter of pessimism or solve it. But I don't see it as a task for men of letters to solve such issues as God, pessimism, etcetera. A literary writer need only portray by whom and in what circumstances God or pessimism were talked about or contemplated. The artist should not judge his characters nor what they say. He should be an impartial witness. I have overheard a haphazard and inconclusive conversation two Russians had on the theme of pessimism. I have to record this conversation in the form in which I heard it. Judgment on this will be passed by the jury, which is the audience. One can only demand of me that I am talented, which means that I am able to distinguish important factors from unimportant ones, that I am able to show the people in their proper light and let them speak their own language.[1]

Chekhov is not interested in "What is pessimism?" nor in "Is this or that theory of pessimism true or untrue, good or bad?" He is interested in the question "How, where and through whom does a certain opinion of pessimism originate, and what has been originated by this opinion?" The writer has to show the constructed nature of the phenomena, ask for the entirety of elements which constitute a phenomenon. Those elements which make it what it is and through which it has the effects it has.

Why should this approach be objective? Not because it preaches the absolute truth about the phenomena involved. If absolute truth does not exist for Chekhov, we can apply the same principle which applies to all statements to his own statements. This is that any statement offers an interpretation of reality which is 'merely' potential, limited and biased by perception.

On the other hand objectivity here seems to imply that the writer must be prepared to stake his own prejudices. In his account there should also be room for elements outside his normal, every-day frame of reference, precisely because these question that framework. He will have to adjust his frame of reference until it accommodates an account which acknowledges anything forgotten or denied, anything hidden and repressed:

> Physicists consider nothing on earth unclean. The writer should be as objective as the physicist. He must cast off his ordinary civilian subjectivity and realize that dung heaps play a very important part in any landscape, and that evil passions are as much a part of life as noble ones.[9]

On the one hand an objective analysis has to show that the whole range of what is not said and not thought is one of the elements constituting a phenomenon. On the other hand this analysis has to show that it is in this range that the problematic nature of the phenomenon most likely manifests itself, where it becomes clear that it violates reality and tries to cover up the conflicts which form the basis of its very existence.

The following quotation can function as a model for the type of account Chekhov strives towards. It is a brief analysis of the function and structure of Sienkiewicz' novels:

> apparently Sienkiewicz has not read Tolstoi, nor is he acquainted with Nietzsche. He talks about hypnotism like a bourgeois citizen, but every page abounds with Rubenses, Borgheses, Corregios and Botticellis. This is to show off his learning in front of the bourgeois reader and to make a face at materialism. The novel aims to put the bourgeoisie to sleep with its dreams of gold. Be faithful to your wife, read your book of prayers together, make money, enjoy sports and your affairs will blossom, in this world as well as in the other. The bourgeoisie love so-called 'positive' types and novels with a happy ending, because these offer the comforting thought that one can gather capital and at the same time maintain one's innocence, that one can be beastly and happy at the same time.[10]

Chekhov shows that Sienkiewicz' novels are not what they seem at first sight. They hide more than they reveal. In a certain sense he discusses them like a symptom, the superficial manifestation of deeper phenomena.

In the first place Chekhov uncovers a number of irrational motives underlying Sienkiewicz' so-called learning. These motives are vanity and a disdain for materialism. Furthermore he reveals that his learning serves to mask great ignorance. Secondly, and perhaps most importantly, Chekhov is aware of the rhetorical function of the novel. According to Chekhov, this function consists of making the reader forget and repress the paradoxical nature of the bourgeois ideology. The novel creates or maintains the illusion that the bourgeoisie is supported and made possible only by 'positive' ideals, such as faith, devoutness, health, material welfare and innocence. But this world of illusions conceals that the bourgeoisie is also constituted by 'negative' elements, such as greed, will to power and injustice.

This clarifies Chekhov's aim in providing an objective explanation. It is the task of the writer to show via an objective explanation of phenomena that these can only be what they are and effect what they effect because they turn one term of any opposition into an absolute and shield off and ignore the opposing term.

In terms of philosophy Chekhov sets out to lay bare the repressive and illusory nature of metaphysical dualism.

Reader and audience attitude

On the basis of the above we can conclude that Chekhov's method is simultaneously critical and non-critical. It is noncritical in that Chekhov refuses to judge the moral nature and degree of truth of the phenomena he describes. But it is critical in the sense that it uncovers what normally remains hidden and shields the problematic aspects of the phenomena from view. Chekhov writes the following to Suvorin:

> You are right in demanding from the artist a conscious attitude towards his work, but you are confusing two things: *solving the question and posing the right question*. The artist should only aspire to the latter.[11]

Chekhov merely wants to form a diagnosis, and offers no therapy. His contemporaries often found this difficult to accept. His objective was not only very innovative, but was also diametrically opposed to the tradition of Russian literature in the second half of the 19th century. This literature was prejudiced and functioned in a sense as a form of political opposition, which in reality was non-existent.[12]

Chekhov wanted to avoid any partiality at all cost. In a letter to Plescheyev he wrote that he feared readers:

who look for tendentiousness between the lines and who want to see me as either liberal or conservative. I am neither liberal, nor conservative, nor gradualist, nor monk, nor indifferentist. [...] Company name and labelling I consider to be prejudices.[13]

Still Chekhov cannot be accused of a lack of commitment. He appeals to his readers to acknowledge the issue he describes and to change their way of life on the basis of this insight. He calls the best writers "real", in the sense that they

> describe (life) as it is, but as each line is permeated, like with juice, with an awareness of its purpose, we feel, apart from life as it is, life as it ought to be, which is what fascinates us.[14]

Chekhov limits himself to undermining and questioning the phenomena he describes by showing how these are constituted by the denial, the oblivion and repression of their paradoxical nature. He does, however, not go any further. He leaves it up to the reader or the audience member to draw whatever conclusions. By way of a contemplation of life as it is (i.e. as Chekhov interprets it) he can come to an insight concerning life as it should be. By negating what is negative reader and audience should reach an expression of what is positive.[15] The recipient of Chekhov's text can no longer remain a passive addressee of a message or moral lesson. He himself has to create the solutions which Chekhov refuses to give. Chekhov chooses this path, not because he is a pessimist, but because he is aware that there is no one truth, but many truths and that one person's truth does not necessarily benefit somebody else.

Parody

I think there is something to be said for viewing Chekhov's work as fundamentally parodical. Parody can be broadly defined as that which copies the original while at the same time undermining and subverting the original by showing it within a ridiculous context. Chekhov too wants to present a copy of phenomena, by imitating, emulating and doubling the actual function and structure of those phenomena as closely as possible.

But just as in parody there is a subtle shift of emphasis, which causes the original to appear in an altered framework, a different context. In Chekhov this context consists of the awareness of the way in which the original is constituted by forgetting and repressing its own paradoxical nature. The change, however small it may seem at first sight, subverts the original, rendering it comical and implausible. Both Chekhov's oeuvre and parody are disrespectful in their respect, and unfaithful in their faithfulness to the original. This paradoxical tension is released in a burst of laughter.[16]

It has taken quite a long time before it was realized that this element of humour is an integrating part of Chekhov's literary aesthetic. Stanislawski and Nemirovic-Danchenko directed Chekhov's plays as tragedies because they did not recognize Chekhov's dialectical view of reality. Nemirovic-Danchenko noted:

> It was during this period that he made the final copy of *The Three Sisters*. We in the theatre read the play in his presence. He fought with his own embarrassment and several times repeated: "I've written a vaudeville piece!" Later he would say the same thing of *The Cherry Orchard*, that he had written a vaudeville piece. Really we could not understand why he called his play that, when on the title of the manuscript he called it a drama. On the other hand; within fifteen or twenty years irresponsible theatrical men would juggle with the phrase.[17]

Both directors did not understand that Chekhov's work contains an ironic, distanced criticism of metaphysical dualism. His comment that *The Three Sisters* and *The Cherry Orchard* are vaudeville plays was meant to stress that the tragic approach of the Moscow Art Theatre neglected the comical nature of his work, an equally important element and inherent to parody.

In this respect I would like to refer to Vera Gottlieb's excellent study, *Chekhov and the Vaudeville*. She discusses an intertextual form of parody that occurs in Chekhov, namely his parodies of the genre of the vaudeville in his one-acts. In literature studies the one-acts are usually regarded as a marginal element of Chekhov's body of work. They are often characterized as vaudeville plays. Gottlieb questions these presumptions in her work.

In the first place she believes that the one-acts are not mere vaudeville pieces, but that they should be regarded as parodical rewrites of the vaudeville. One of the aims of this rewriting was to make the audience aware of the nature and function of this genre while at the same time undermining it.

Chekhov shows that the vaudeville (and by implication the other traditional genres such as tragedy and comedy) consist of worn-out traditions which do not offer a satisfactory picture of reality. Chekhov questions the underlying ideological structures and shows how these distort reality. On the one hand one may say he is taking apart the conventions. On the other hand Chekhov creates a new text on the basis of this 'waste material'. In this new text the conflicts and paradoxes emerge which before have been suppressed by the traditional literary forms or which have been wrongly presented as reconcilable.

Secondly Gottlieb demonstrates that the one-acts function as a kind of 'pilot'-pieces to the later full-length plays. As suggested, this occurs in and by means of parody, in and by means of the different use Chekhov makes of the vaudeville conventions. Thus he creates new techniques which he can use to give shape to the paradoxes of reality. The techniques he uses in the full-length plays are identical to or derived from the techniques he designed in the one-acts.

The one-acts link Chekhov's great works for the stage to the traditions of vaudeville and comedy. They are a kind of laboratory where Chekhov designs and develops his techniques and puts them to the test, before or after applying them in the full-length plays.

This point of view has clear implications. If we want to fully understand the genealogy of Chekhov's work, we should investigate how and to what extent Chekhov was influenced by comedy and vaudeville in his one-act plays. We should also determine how this reception affected the other parts of his work. I will refrain from illustrating the fruitfulness of this approach with examples. I would like to refer again to Vera Gottlieb's book, and in particular to the second chapter which offers a detailed description of her findings concerning these matters.[18]

Chekhov and the realistic/naturalistic tradition

We have come to the point where we can answer the question to what extent Chekhov's work is compatible with the tradition of realism and naturalism. On the basis of the analysis given above I think that Chekhov's work does not qualify as an exponent of this tradition.

First, Chekhov's thought is characterized by strong doubt in matters of epistemological concern. In realism and naturalism it is still held that we can describe and explain reality objectively on the basis of our knowledge. Chekhov considers this to be a pretension based on illusions.

Human thought is by definition imperfect. It can never entirely comprehend all the meanings and effects it generates. There always is a surplus of meanings and effects, and these undermine whatever an interpretation attempts to say and do.

Chekhov's parodies are aimed at refuting the claim to an absolute truth upheld by the phenomena which are the subject of parody, by showing in what way this claim is constituted by repressing and forgetting the paradoxical nature of reality.

Secondly realism and naturalism demand from actor as well as audience a complete identification with the character on the stage and with the dilemma of the play. The audience is supposed to immerse itself and to give in to the illusion that the world of fiction is real.

This immersion operates to a certain degree in Chekhov, but at the same time the identification of audience member with a character is interrupted by a critical and distanced approach. In daily life, as well as in realism and naturalism, the audience experiences reality only in the light of metaphysical dualism. Chekhov, on the other hand, reveals that any term in a series of oppositions can only be made absolute by forgetting and repressing the opposite term. His parodies reveal the problematic nature of conventional interpretations and force reader and audience to reconsider their position concerning those interpretations.

Finally there is a third difference. In realism and naturalism theatre is a vehicle for some or other moral lesson or message. This is no longer the case with Chekhov. As stated above, he always refused to offer solutions for the problems he identified. The reader, by way of negating the negative, has to come up with the positive solutions which Chekhov denies him out of democratic respect for the reader's individuality and state of being.

Notes

* The lecture by Herta Schmid, 'Waiting for Stanislavsky – The Situation of the Russian Theatre as a Result of Utopian and Realistic Reforms', was to our regret not available for publication in this volume.

1. Vera Gottlieb, *Chekhov and the Vaudeville. A Study of Chekhov's One-Act Plays* (Cambridge: Cambridge University Press, 1982).

2. Vera Gottlieb, p. 1.

3. This definition of Hegel's philosophy is inspired by Peter V. Zima, *Literarische Ästhetik. Methoden und Modelle der Literaturwissenschaft* (Tübingen: Francke Verlag, 1991), pp. 24-25 and 42.

4. From a letter to A.S. Suvorin, dated May 30, 1888, in: A.P. Tsjechow, *Verzamelde Werken, Notities en Brieven* vol. 7, trans. Tom Eekman. (Amsterdam: G.A. van Oorschot, 1956) (De Russische Bibliotheek), pp. 154-5.

5. This interpretation of Kuprin's quote is suggested by Vera Gottlieb, p. 1.

6. From a letter to A.S. Suvorin, dated October 27, 1888, in: Tsjechow, p. 197.

7. *Ibidem.*

8. From a letter to A.S. Suvorin, dated May 30, 1888, in: Tsjechow, p. 154.

9. From a letter to M.W. Kiselewa, dated January 14, 1887, in: Tsjechow, p. 98.

10. From a letter to A.S. Suvorin, dated April 13, 1895, in: Tsjechow, p. 415.

11. From a letter to A.S. Suvorin, dated October 27, 1888, in: Tsjechow, p. 197.

12. I. Dlugosch, *Anton Pavlovic Cechov und das Theater des Absurden* (München: Wilhelm Fink Verlag, 1977), p. 244.

13. From a letter to A.N. Plescheyev, dated October 4, 1888, in: Tsjechow, p. 179.

14. From a letter to A.S. Suvorin, dated November 25, 1892, in: Tsjechow, p. 365.

15. I. Dlugosch, p. 256.

16. The definition of parody is inspired by P. Moyaert, 'Jacques Derrida en de filosofie van de differentie,' in: S. IJsseling (ed.), *Jacques Derrida. Een inleiding in zijn denken* (Baarn: Ambo, 1986), pp. 34-5.

17. V. Nemirovic-Danchenko, *My Life in Russian Theatre*, trans. John Cournos (New York: Theatre Art Books, 1968), p. 209.

18. I am referring to the chapter 'Conventions and innovations in Russian comedy,' in: Vera Gottlieb, pp. 12-45.

Henri Behar, Université de la Sorbonne Nouvelle, U.F.R. de Littérature et Linguistique françaises et latines, 13, rue Santeuil, 75005 Paris, France.

Jean Chothia, Selwyn College, Grange Road, Cambridge CB3-9DQ, UK.

Rob Erenstein, Universiteit van Amsterdam, Vakgroep Theaterwetenschap, Nieuwe Doelenstraat 16, 1012 CP Amsterdam, The Netherlands.

Christa Hasche, Humboldt-Universität, Institut für Theaterwissenschaft, Fachbereich Kultur- und Kunstwissenschaft, Universitätsstraße 3-B, 10099 Berlin, Germany.

Karel Hupperetz, Rijksuniversiteit Groningen, Vakgroep Muziek- en Theaterwetenschap, Postbus 716, 9700 AS Groningen, The Netherlands.

Mary Kemperink, Rijksuniversiteit Groningen, Vakgroep Nederlands, Postbus 716, 9700 AS Groningen, The Netherlands.

Ivo Kuyl, Moesstraat 9-D, 9717 JT Groningen, The Netherlands.

Henk van der Liet, Rijksuniversiteit Groningen, Vakgroep Scandinavische Talen en Culturen, Postbus 716, 9700 AS Groningen, The Netherlands.

Hans van Maanen, Rijksuniversiteit Groningen, Vakgroep Muziek- en Theaterwetenschap, Postbus 716, 9700 AS Groningen, The Netherlands.

Frank Salaün, Rijksuniversiteit Groningen, Vakgroep Romaanse Talen en Culturen, Postbus 716, 9700 AS Groningen, The Netherlands.

Serge Salaün, Université de la Sorbonne Nouvelle, U.F.R. Etudes Ibériques et Latino-américaines, 13, rue Santeuil, 75005 Paris, France.

Egil Törnqvist, Universiteit van Amsterdam, Skandinavisch Seminarium, Spuistraat 134, 1012 VB Amsterdam, The Netherlands.

Margot Versteeg, Rijksuniversiteit Groningen, Vakgroep Romaanse Talen en Culturen, Postbus 716, 9700 AS Groningen, The Netherlands.

Helen Wilcox, Rijksuniversiteit Groningen, Vakgroep Engels, Postbus 716, 9700 AS Groningen, The Netherlands.